W9-BIN-036

CULTURE SHOCK!

United Arab Emirates

Gina L. Crocetti

Graphic Arts Center Publishing Company
Portland, Oregon

In the same series

Australia	Hong Kong	Philippines	London at Your Door
Bolivia	India	Singapore	Paris at Your Door
Borneo	Indonesia	South Africa	Rome at Your Door
Britain	Ireland	Spain	
Burma	Israel	Sri Lanka	A Globe-Trotter's Guide
California	Italy	Sweden	A Parent's Guide
Canada	Japan	Switzerland	A Student's Guide
Chile	Korea	Syria	A Traveller's Medical Guide
China	Laos	Taiwan	A Wife's Guide
Cuba	Malaysia	Thailand	Living and Working Abroad
Czech	Mauritius	Turkey	Working Holidays Abroad
Republic	Mexico	USA	
Denmark	Morocco	USA—The	
Egypt	Nepal	South	
France	Netherlands	Vietnam	
Germany	Norway		
Greece	Pakistan		

Illustrations by TRIGG

© 1996 Times Editions Pte Ltd
Reprinted 1998

This book is published by special
arrangement with Times Editions Pte Ltd
Times Centre, 1 New Industrial Road, Singapore 536196
International Standard Book Number 1-55868-300-3
Library of Congress Catalog Number 96-77208
Graphic Arts Center Publishing Company
P.O. Box 10306 • Portland, Oregon 97296-0306 • (503) 226-2402

Printed in Singapore

The Hidden Culture

The traveller may stay at this level as long as the sojourn lasts, be it one week or many years, but it is a surface level existence only. Layers of contradictions that are annoying at first are soon incorporated into a person's character, making life that much easier. An inner clock sets itself to the five daily prayer calls. *Insha'alla* (God willing) becomes an automatic thought when someone predicts the future. Life is perceived from modern to traditional and the transition between familiar modern conveniences and unchanging, ceaseless traditions is made constantly and with ease.

The Emirati culture and society are almost completely hidden from the larger expatriate population by high walls, tinted windows, and layers of wealth. Foreigners may well acquaint themselves with people from any number of cultures: Scottish, Indian, Russian or Asian, but eventually, the question might be asked, "Where are the people indigenous to the area?" Many books have been written about them by British authors who passed long periods in the culture when the country was newly formed. But unless visitors' jobs directly associate them with the Emiratis (teaching for example), they are unlikely to pass much time with the natives.

You will, however, live by many of their customs and most certainly by their laws. Your life in this liberal Muslim country will be comfortable and your family will be relatively safe from the ills of a modern world. You will find an active community life, friends and much to occupy your free time, yet life has a surprising unreality to it and as long as one stays, it remains a tangible unreality. Therein lies the mystic lure of Arabia proclaimed in movies such as *The Desert Song* and *Lawrence of Arabia*. But the desert mirages have not disappeared, rather, like everything else, they have adapted themselves to modern life.

The UAE is a country moving ahead as hard as it is attempting to stand still. The Emiratis have travelled centuries in the last two and a half decades. Charming and hospitable, they are spanning a long bridge of time and are doing so on their own terms. While the Emirati has incorporated modern methods and conveniences into daily life, the expatriate is constantly struck by the contradictions created in the juxtaposition of a modern world on a traditional society. Accepting and respecting the Emiratis' terms and the frequent contradictions will help enrich the cultural experience. It is to those who wish to look below the surface appearances, to meet the people and to understand why things are what they are that this book is aimed.

LOCATION

The country is located on the Persian Gulf, across from Iran. Its bordering neighbours are Oman to the south, Saudi Arabia to the south and southwest, and Qatar to the west. The entire country is 83,600 square kilometres (33,400 square miles), about the size of Austria. It is made up of seven territories called emirates. Abu Dhabi is the largest of the emirates and with 71,000 square kilometres (28,400 square miles) comprises about 85% of the territory. Ajman is

The occasional oasis belies the otherwise hostile environment of the desert.

the smallest with just over 250 square kilometres (100 square miles). The country has 1,000 kilometres (620 miles) of coastline on the Persian Gulf and 130 kilometres (80 miles) of coastline on the Gulf of Oman.

Most of the country's land is barren desert. There are huge rolling sand dunes along the Saudi Arabian border and low, hard-packed foothills on the Oman border. There are a few oases (fertile spots with enough water to make some agriculture possible): a large one is in Buraimi and Al-Ain, along the Oman border and there is a string of small ones in Liwa. Salt flats are found along the coasts.

In Ras al-Khaimah further north, the soil is quite fertile, making it the breadbasket of the country. The northern part of the Hajar mountains of Oman runs through the UAE dividing Fujairah from the other emirates. There is some above ground evidence of the earth's plate movement hundreds of thousands of years ago. Jebel Hafeet, a solitary and crumbly limestone mountain hovering 1,340 metres (4,420 feet) above the inland city of Al-Ain is covered with shellfish and small plant fossils – evidence it was once below sea level.

CLIMATE

The climate of the UAE is uncomfortably hot and humid for about five months in the summer (mid May–September). Temperatures are usually in the low 40s (Celsius – around 104°F) but may sometimes reach higher than 50°C (122°F). Summer months are made even less pleasant by the coastal humidity. Many of the nationals keep summer homes inland in Al-Ain or Liwa to escape the humidity. The mountains also afford some relief to people in the northern emirates and air conditioned houses, offices, shops, and cars offer virtually nonstop relief from the heat to city residents. Ocean temperatures are high in summer, around 35°C (95°F) but they can go higher. When they do, the water is hotter than the body's temperature and a swim is no longer refreshing.

Temperatures the rest of the year are quite pleasant. The days are clear and warm and the nights are cool. Inland temperatures can drop drastically at night to below 10°C (50°F) in winter.

The UAE is geologically stable and well sheltered within the Persian Gulf. Thus, other than the relentless heat, it does not suffer major natural phenomena such as earthquakes, eruptions or typhoons.

Rainfall

The UAE averages less than 10 inches (25 centimetres) of rain a year. In a year when rain falls, it will usually do so from August to September and/or January to February. The rainfall can be characterised into three categories. The first is the one that never materialises. Clouds gather in the afternoon, the sky spits and the clouds move, bypassing the country. The second is the most useful. Again clouds gather in the afternoon, the wind builds up and there is a tremendous, short-lived storm, throwing sand and anything loose where it pleases. Then the sun comes out and it is as hot as ever. This rainfall will occur several days in a row again and again through August and September. It is exciting as it changes day into night and the desert into a garden.

The last kind of rainfall is a dangerous one. Clouds gather and remain for days dumping tons of water. The sand absorbs just enough to cement into a hard-packed floor. Water accumulates on the surface and as it increases it gains force until the earth cannot bear its weight, crumbles away and a canyon is torn into the earth's surface. Water rushes down the new canyon carrying with it anything in its path, including people, animals, cars and houses. This type of canyon is called a *wadi*. Its newly formed walls afford enough shade for vegetation to grow and it will often carry a permanent trickle of water in it. Very old, permanent wadis have settlements near them and seeking newly formed wadis is a source of entertainment now that four-wheel-drive (4WD) vehicles make the trip across the desert fairly simple. 1996 was an exceptional year, with nearly three straight months of rainfall. The transformation of the desert from brown to green was astounding.

Although the average rainfall in the Emirates is quite low, flooding can occur when sudden storms strike.

POPULATION DISTRIBUTION

The latest internal census published in the *Gulf News* in January, 1996 listed the population of the UAE at almost 2.4 million. That makes a 45% increase in 10 years. According to the *Country Guide* published by the Library of Congress in the U.S., only 12% of the residents are actually nationals. These nationals are Arab Muslims, predominantly of the Sunni sect, and are referred to as Emiratis. Westerners make up 5–10% of the population; non-national Arabs comprise 10–15%; and the remaining 60–70% are primarily labourers from India, Pakistan, Baluchistan, Afghanistan, and the Philippines.

With the exceptions of the Indian and Filipino populations, nearly all members of the labour group are men. People tend to form friendships and ties with people of the same or similar nationalities. Each nationality then manages to live to a large degree according to the norms and values of his or her homeland. The high numbers of expatriates as compared to nationals is alarming and its impact is significant. The ratio of men to women (as much as 4/5:1) is also significant and permeates many aspects of the culture.

15

Early Contact

The UAE, conveniently located on a major trade route, has been inhabited since the third millennium B.C. The first known group of people were the Umm An-Nar who settled on the island of Abu Dhabi and whose civilisation extended to the coast of Oman. They were probably fishermen but little is actually known about them. They are thought to be unrelated to the famous Dilmun Empire which was recently discovered to have been located nearby.

After the Umm An-Nar civilisation came the Greeks who settled for a short time in the northern emirates, probably for trade purposes. Trade continued in the area throughout the Bronze Age. The Islamic era followed the Bronze Age. Islam began in this era and then spread to all parts of the Arabian world, India, and countries around the Mediterranean.

During the middle ages, the area formed part of the Kingdom of Hormuz. This group had control of the entrance to the Gulf and gave it the name Straits of Hormuz. The Portuguese followed and stayed from about 1500–1630. They left their woodworking handicraft as a legacy. One may occasionally come across an old Portuguese chest in the market places of Oman or the UAE (Most likely though the pieces are newly constructed and made to look old). These pieces can come with a very high price tag. Because of its constant contact with other cultures through trade, influences are seen in many aspects of the Emirati culture, from available items to types of food and the genetic legacy. The Portuguese were driven out by forces both on land and at sea. The British and Dutch attacked with their fleets at sea while a tribe from Oman, called the Al-Busaid, came by land. Persia was also a contender for the land for a time in the mid 18th century.

British Presence

Modern history in the UAE begins with the British using their naval power to take a stronger hold of the area. While the British battled their way in by sea, two local tribes were gaining in size and power.

One was the Qawasim tribe and the other the Bani Yas. Four of today's emirs can trace their ancestors to these two tribes.

The Qawasim were seafarers who settled in what is today Ras al-Khaimah. They fought and pushed out the Persians, who were coming at them from Iran, and the Al-Busaids, the tribe invading from Oman. The Al-Busaids were fighting to keep the French out of Oman at the same time the Qawasims were pushing at their back door. The Al-Busaids enlisted the aid of the British to keep this new presence out. This move was perceived by the Qawasims as an alliance with the enemy and they declared war on Britain, attacking British ships as they pleased. The British East India company thought this was piracy and dubbed the area the Pirate Coast.

In the early 1800s Britain retaliated with its own raids on the ships owned by the Qawasim but was unable to alter the situation. Then, in 1820 Britain came into the Gulf and destroyed or captured every Qawasim ship they could find and occupied Qawasim territory in Ras al-Khaimah and Persia. The British then imposed a peace treaty on the Arab tribes in the area. The treaty made it illegal for the Arabs to attack the British but allowed the tribes to attack each other. The tribes did attack each other with a relish distasteful to the British who repeatedly modified the treaty over the years in an effort to bring about a lasting peace. In 1853, the Treaty of Peace in Perpetuity was imposed making the British arbitrators of disputes between the sheikhs of warring tribes. The Pirate Coast became known as the Trucial Coast after the ensuing truce interventions that had to be imposed over the years.

The Oil Boom and Decolonisation

With the discovery of oil in the 1940s and 1950s, Britain established an even stronger presence to protect this financial interest. Several British subjects were personally interested in the Arabs and their welfare. They lived with the Emiratis, wrote many books about them, and generally educated much of the world about these people. In 1968, in a political post-World War II climate favouring decolonisation,

Britain pulled back and encouraged the Emiratis to form an independent country. Britain withdrew politically and militarily. She did so with good will and in a positive climate.

Another factor in Britain's withdrawal was the rise of Arab nationalism. The British had learned that military force was not effective with the Arabs and the way to guarantee British and other foreign enterprise in the Gulf was through negotiation and mutual respect of rights – not through military force. In daily life this applies also, as you will find calmness and negotiation serve you much better than losing your temper. Today, Britain's financial interests in the area are strong and many of her subjects are gainfully employed in the UAE in the oil industry and other fields.

When the emirates formed their federation, the neighbouring countries of Bahrain and Qatar were invited to join. Both opted to remain independent

LEADERSHIP

In the past, each family belonged to one of seven tribes. Each tribe elected a sheikh, usually the most respected and admired man of the tribe. This man followed tribal opinion rather than imposed duties and arbitrated rather than commanded. He was advised by a council of elders. His own cleverness assisted him in settling disputes as well and caused him to be admired by his people even more.

Tribes fought each other to gain territory and power over one another. Rivalry among the tribes kept territorial boundaries shifting and some boundaries are still not clear today. Boundaries that are still under dispute are marked with dotted lines on maps. Today, unclear boundaries exist with Oman and Saudi Arabia. The boundaries are left unclear rather than risk a serious dispute.

While the sheikh was the lawful ruler and leader, the *mutawa* was the community's religious leader. He led the people in reciting the Holy Koran *(Quran or Qura'an)* and it was through this medium that literacy was gained. Life for the Emiratis was difficult, steeped in thousand year old traditions, and such luxuries as formal education were barely even concepts. The country and the people remained entirely unexposed to a developing world until the middle of this century.

Today, the UAE is a federation of seven Arab states or emirates. These are Abu Dhabi, Dubai, Sharjah, Ras al-Khaimah, Ajman, Umm al-Qaiwain, and Fujairah. Each emirate is named after its main town or city and is controlled politically and economically by its sheikh. The federal government (called the Supreme Council), led by H. H. Sheikh Zayed bin Sultan al Nahyan of Abu Dhabi, controls the country's foreign affairs, defence and the federation's economic and social development. Sheikh Zayed came to power in Abu Dhabi in 1966 and has been the country's president since its founding on December 2, 1971. One of the council's jobs is to elect a new president every five years and their consistency in choosing the same man each time speaks for Sheikh Zayed's popularity.

Below the Supreme Council there is a Cabinet. Most of the Cabinet posts are held by men from Abu Dhabi and Dubai in consideration for contributing the most money to the federal government. In addition to the Supreme Council and the Cabinet there is a National Council made up of forty members. Members are appointed by the Sheikhs and appointments tend to go to family members based on relationships and favours rather than on qualifications. This was a problem in the past when qualifications were questionable, but this is less so now that the nationals are formally educated. The National Council advises the other two political entities but cannot overrule them.

THE RULERS

'Emir' or 'Sheikh' are words meaning prince. They are used to refer to the rulers, however, the honorific 'Sheikh' is preferred in the Emirates ('Sheikha' for the wives of the rulers). The current rulers are:

Abu Dhabi – Sheikh Zayed Bin Sultan al-Nahyan

Dubai – Sheikh Maktoum bin Rashid al-Maktoum

Sharjah – Sheikh Sultan Bin Mohammed al-Qasimi

Ras al-Khaimah – Sheikh Saqr Bin Mohammed al-Qasimi

Ajman – Sheikh Humaid Bin Rashid al-Nuaimi

Umm al-Qaiwain – Sheikh Rashid Bin Ahmad al-Mualla

Fujairah – Sheikh Hamad Bin Mohammed al-Sharqi

The Benevolent Ruler and a Welfare State

One means to a stable economy is a stable political system. The UAE has had the same ruler since its inception as a country and, as a result, has had peace and a healthy economy throughout its short history.

Sheikh Zayed won his people's loyalty through educating them, providing them with an infrastructure, and by sharing responsibilities of his new government with his family members and the youth of the country. His popularity permeates every aspect of life. All businesses large and small, government or private, post his picture in the front office; newspapers carry front page reports on him daily no matter how insignificant the news; and nationals and non-nationals alike speak respectfully and lovingly about him. Nearly every book you find about the Emirates will have a full page picture of Sheikh Zayed inside the front cover and his photograph is the first you will see upon arrival in the country. You may be prevented from entering hotels where he is staying or delayed in driving to a destination if his retinue is passing. In such a small country, unexpectedly coming into such close contact with the ruler is inevitable.

Sheikh Zayed has done much financially to earn his popularity. He has provided his countrymen with comfortable housing; excellent, free medical care; education (either at the one university in Al-Ain or full funding for studies abroad); and new roads between each of the emirates. He has also secured concessions from foreign oil companies that assure the country's high earnings; kept peace in the region for

Ruler of the United Arab Emirates, Sheikh Zayed bin Sultan al Nahyan of Abu Dhabi. He has ruled the Emirates since the country was founded in 1971.

two and a half decades; and provided jobs for nationals who want them. The nationals work primarily in high management and government positions.

The 'real' work is done by the expatriates and is managed by the nationals. A new generation has the biggest, best, and newest of everything without really having had to work for it. As a result, this newly prosperous society is losing its traditional values. Because of its new prosperity, rapid change is occurring and the area has become a welfare state in the truest sense of the expression. However, unlike other welfare systems, the recipients of the funds are the top echelon of society who view everyone else as paid 'servants.' (The impact of this will be addressed in Chapter Two.) It will be up to history to judge the Emiratis' decision to embrace modernisation so completely as being right or wrong, good or bad, or the best or worst they could have done.

THE LAW

It is proper that a private harm be borne to avert a public harm
—UAE law, Article 105

There are two laws – tribal law which people morally adhere to, and Islamic law which the government enforces. Tribal laws are the shared beliefs of the Emiratis which form the moral fibre of their society and which are very much in keeping with their Islamic beliefs. The moral code is the slowest to change as it is in any culture. Tribal law is stronger than modern law. It prevents people from committing crimes because of the repercussions of its harsh punishment. Previously, a crime committed against the tribe resulted in banishment, subsequent isolation and certain death. Tribal law governs the relations of husband to wife, parents to children, man to man, and tribe to tribe. They are explained in more detail in the chapters on Family and Values (see Chapters Four and Six).

Islamic Law

Islamic law is taken from four sources: *Shariah*, *Sunnah*, *Ijma*, and *Qiyas*. Shariah law comes directly from the Koran. It is perhaps the most important of the four sources because it is the most frequently consulted and provides the largest source of guidance. The other three are consulted to confirm and support Shariah law or else to provide answers for questions Shariah law does not address.

The second source, Sunnah law, is the collection of the prophets' deeds and utterances which have been passed down through the generations. Thirdly, there is Ijma law which is derived from the consensus of solutions to religious problems not addressed in Shariah law or Sunnah law. Finally, there is Qiyas law which is assigned by reasoning through analogy when decisions cannot be made based on the other three laws. Law in the Emirates is referred to as Shariah law no matter what source is consulted and the court is known as Shariah court.

Those who stand trial in Shariah court are innocent until proven guilty by the accuser. Four eyewitnesses are required for the accuser to prove guilt. Both parties can appeal to a higher court if they are dissatisfied with the proceedings. Only the parties involved in a dispute appear in court because there is no jury, just the judge. If the judge cannot make a decision, he may ask the defendant to take an oath swearing his innocence. Christians take a Christian oath and Muslims take a Muslim one. If the defendant refuses to take the oath, he is automatically found guilty. This solution works for the Emiratis because to lie under oath will condemn the guilty person to the eternal fires of hell and they cannot imagine anyone risking that.

As of yet, there are no federal criminal laws. Such laws are in a developmental stage, but are taking a while to complete, since laws must be agreed to by the majority of the rulers. There is currently a civil criminal code to address crimes committed by expatriates. This code is slightly different for each emirate, but is fashioned after Western concepts of law. Westerners are most likely to be tried under this law while nationals and other Muslims are usually tried in the Sharia court. There are exceptions depending on what the offence is and who is offended. Proceedings usually tried in Sharia court are homicide, divorce and rape. Shariah law metes harsh punishments. Sexual offences such as adultery are subject to lashing or stoning. Murder and rape are punishable by death by hanging or firing squad.

While Shariah law is not usually applied to Westerners who commit crimes, it does happen. Westerners who commit crimes are usually only deported. However, they can be tried according to Sharia law without their national embassy being able to intervene.

The Emiratis usually turn a blind eye and a deaf ear to expatriates' activities. They do not wish to stir up political strife on the one hand, but on the other they firmly believe in tolerance of other people's beliefs. Still, there are no guarantees and you need to be aware that you do not have the same rights in this country as you may have in your home country. Most criminal proceedings for Westerners are crimes that involve alcohol. Punishments encompass lashings, prison terms, fines, or a combination of these.

A large percentage of non-Western expatriates are Muslim. They are automatically tried in Shariah court. Their crimes are well publicised and in those accounts, the crime is frequently sensationalised. By portraying the criminal as a monster, killing them for their crime is made easier. The world sees an account of a Filipino or Indian maid executed for killing her Emirati master who was raping her. She may well have been without choices in the situation, but she is also responsible for her actions. It is a harsh law in a country that has known a harsh existence.

ECONOMICS

Eighty percent of the Emirate's income comes from royalties paid by internationally owned oil producing companies. They have few other natural resources (fishing and pearling) but the revenues from oil enable their healthy economy to flourish. At one time they had one of the highest per capita incomes in the world. While incomes are still healthy, inflation has caught up and the fantastic salaries of a few years ago are fewer.

Abu Dhabi is the largest and wealthiest emirate and it has the largest population. As a result, it dominates the federation. Abu Dhabi desires strong integration of the seven emirates while the other six emirates wish to retain some degree of independence and autonomy. At the same time they do not wish to lose the financial generosity of Abu Dhabi. Dubai is the second largest, wealthiest and most populated of the emirates. In addition to oil revenues, Dubai gets revenue from its trading industry. Tourism is the third main revenue producing industry and again affects Abu Dhabi and Dubai more than the other emirates which do not have as much to offer in the way of comfort, entertainment and variety. The other emirates do not have the economic growth of Abu Dhabi and Dubai, they are also not as subject to social change. Those desiring more of a cultural experience will want to find work in these emirates.

Growing Pains

The primary new source of income that the UAE has been seeking to expand is tourism. To date, this new industry is a great success. Over 100,000 visitors come to the Emirates every year to partake of the wonderful winter weather, to experience a setting remarkably different from their own, and to shop in the numerous market places. But allowing tourism forces a conservative Muslim people to allow alcohol consumption, religious and racial freedom, and English as the unofficial common language in their own country. This social freedom forces the Emiratis to face such problems as prostitution, drug smuggling, and illegal immigration, to name only a few. While the Emiratis allow a liberal lifestyle in their country, they do not allow it for themselves. Severe punishment is meted out to the Muslim, regardless of nationality, breaking the laws of Islam.

Another new source of income the Emiratis are after is imposing tariffs and taxes where none existed before. They have not yet been implemented but when they are, the Emiratis themselves will be exempt while the foreign population will be detrimentally affected by them. Expatriates have been able to earn healthy tax-free incomes to date, but the Emiratis have been gradually lowering the salaries they pay foreigners. They have been successful in doing so without chasing away foreign workers because the Emirates can be such a pleasant place to live and many people are willing to take jobs that pay less in order to live there.

FORESIGHT

Sheikh Zayed began a campaign to educate his people before the emirates even formed a country. In the 1950s, with the financial assistance of the other Arabic countries, the Emiratis were able to establish their first elementary and high schools. Graduates then went abroad for a university education and returned with the qualifications to run government departments and the police force. Other countries continued to send teachers to the area and the Emiratis' have been able to continue the development of their educational system.

Sheikh Zayed also believes it is necessary to educate the Emirati women. Since the population of Emiratis is so small, and their rate of development so great, women are needed to help run the country. Few Emirati women are actually in the workforce yet and those who are, are placed in high management positions where they are less likely to come into contact with men or be in situations that might compromise their reputation. The Emirates have one university that opened in 1972. It has a separate women's campus. The quality of education at the university improves every year and it is gaining quite a good reputation. Muslim parents from all over the Middle East try to get their daughters admitted to the university because they can be sure their daughters will be cloistered behind walls without access to members of the opposite sex, drugs, and anything else that might affect their reputation.

The Sheikh's wife, Sheikha Fatima, has embarked on a campaign to educate the older generation. Adult literacy classes are available for the Emiratis in the larger cities.

Education has continued to be a primary development goal. It is an important force in accelerating cultural and political change. This has proven true for many countries and is doing so in the Emirates. In the past, the teacher was the main element in maintaining traditions. Now the teacher, who often comes from abroad, is the agent of change.

Chapter Two

THE EMIRATIS

A CROSS SECTION

The United Arab Emirates is a distinctly international country. An estimated 85% of the country's two million residents are non-UAE nationals. By far the largest group of foreigners are the labourers. They come mainly from the Indian subcontinent and Asia and comprise roughly 60-65% of the population. Non-Gulf Arabs come to work in the Emirates from Egypt, Syria, Palestine, Lebanon, Jordan, and North Africa. They make up about 10–15% of the population. Westerners, those people from native-English speaking countries and from western Europe, comprise 5% of the population. Many estimates put the percentage of Emiratis at 15–20% but this is probably high.

Labourer in a gold souk (market). This man's job is to transport goods from the docks to the markets. Foreign labourers have little status in the Emirates.

All people are not equal. Status is awarded according to national-ity and is portrayed most obviously in work opportunities. Low status jobs involve manual labour. White collar work is awarded higher status. Education can help elevate a person within their group but cannot elevate anyone to a higher status group. A Westerner believing himself to be above such stratification and treating all people as equal will run into trouble. Not only is the structure imposed by higher status groups, it is also accepted by the lower status groups. When you treat someone of lower status as equal to you, they may interpret your friendliness as sexual interest and availability. This applies to both men and women.

This chapter begins with a description of the host culture in order to illustrate the overall environment the foreigner can expect to find. Following that is a general description of the different foreign population groups, though they are not in order according to their status. A few things to keep in mind are that each foreign group is a little different in the Emirates than they would be in their own country. Thus an Indian in the UAE does not necessarily behave the same as an Indian in India, just as the Egyptian in the Emirates is different to the typical Egyptian, and so on. The descriptions below are general and not based on in-depth study of each individual group, rather it is an expatriate view of those groups in this environment. Within each group description are comments on their occupations and their home life, along with advice for interacting with them.

THE BEDOUIN

The Emiratis have been (and many still are) a nomadic group of people referred to as *Bedouin* or *Bedu* for short. They travelled in family groups, tending their herds of sheep, goats, and camels, raiding other tribes and seeking sources of fresh water. These tribes ranged in size from a few to thousands. They grouped together for protection from other warring tribes. Contact with another Bedouin tribe could be cause for celebration or dispute over territorial boundaries.

The Bedu were born into one of three classes: royalty, the middle class, or the lower class. One was born into one of these classes and found it possible to change to another only by gaining power over other tribes or by marrying into one of the royal families. Today's royal family is quite large and in high profile in the news. Their wealth is practically obscene and seemingly capable of moving the earth.

Most of the Emiratis who are not royalty belong to the next class, the middle class. This class is quite well to do by the standards of most countries. Many expatriates belong to a middle class due to their professional knowledge, experience, expertise, education and income. This middle class membership is financial and has no relation to social mores.

Finally, the lower and largest class is comprised mainly of labourers who find themselves rich by the standards of their country but poor in the Emirates. There are Emiratis who are not well to do particularly in the villages, but their financial and social status is still higher than that of the labourers.

The Majlis

It is said that where two or more gather to share coffee and conversation there is a *majlis*. The majlis, an area for meeting, is the most important defined space in an Emirati home or settlement. It is a tent or room in a house having wall to wall carpeting and large, firm pillows on the floor. Guests are entertained in this room. There may be two of these rooms, one for the men and one for the women. The women gather in the majlis daily to gossip, trade stories, jokes, and medicinal remedies and children learn the difference between right and wrong and how to bring honour rather than shame to the family through the majlis talk. Even the rulers of the Emirates meet in a majlis to discuss the business of running the country.

A room is not required for the majlis to take place. The desert floor makes a nice seat particularly if there is also shade nearby and a seated group of men sharing a thermos of coffee on a roundabout at a fairly busy intersection of town is not an uncommon sight.

Bedouin Lifestyle

The Bedu's easily constructed houses were made of palm fronds or blankets forming a tent with an open side. Carpets were laid on the sand to serve as the floor. Camels and goats from their herds provided

Two Emirati men drinking coffee in a majlis, an important social custom of Arab culture which places great importance on hospitality.

milk, meat and wool for shelter and clothing. Meat came also from gazelles the men hunted or from the bustard, an indigenous bird the men caught with the aid of their falcons. Dates were taken from date palms growing in wadis, but the active cultivation of agriculture was never a main source of food.

Some Bedouins settled more permanently in particularly fertile spots near wadis. Here their houses were built of dried mud. Houses were small and rectangular with a short, narrow wood door for an entry way. These narrow doors made it difficult for an unwanted intruder to force his way in. Food was still provided by the Bedu's herds and by hunting, but an irrigation system called a *falaj* was also developed and these more permanent settlers began growing some crops.

31

Today there are still Bedouin in the Emirates. They sometimes roam the desert on the backs of their camels but may also tend their herds in a Toyota Land Cruiser. Most likely though, they have hired subcontinent labourers to tend the herds. They earn a healthy living by raising camels for racing. A good racing camel is worth between 40,000 and 100,000 dirham (dh) – the UAE currency, (about US$15,000–$30,000). The government often fronts the cash prizes at races so even the once self-sufficient Bedu is a recipient in the welfare state. Bedouin have not entirely given up raiding. They breed their camels with herds they come across in the desert. Wild camels do not exist in the Emirates, all are owned. However, they are allowed to freely graze anywhere. You will encounter them on forays away from the cities. They are fairly docile animals and very well protected by law. (See Chapter Seven for more on camels.)

You may encounter a 'Bedouin' in a hotel lobby. He is hired by the hotel to provide a majlis-like atmosphere for guests. This man sits in the foyer, serves the guests traditional coffee and tells stories of traditional life. He probably takes a taxi to his air-conditioned, concrete constructed home at the end of the day. You might also meet a Bedouin in court if you have hit one of his livestock with your car.

Finally, if you go to the non-touristy, traditional markets, you will see the Bedouin men buying and selling livestock and the women selling bags and harnesses made from the wool from their herds. These Bedouin have had the least contact with Westerners and their lives have been least affected by modern changes of all the Emiratis. You will be as much of a curiosity to them as they are to you. A friend of mine was so delighted with three older women we stumbled across who were weaving their goods, she sat and watched them for a while. The women were curious about her and they chatted away together not understanding a word of the other's language. My friend finally bought a camel bag from them and uses it for holding potatoes. The occasions when you do see Bedouin are rare and light as was this encounter.

THE MODERN EMIRATI

Most Emiratis now live in modern, single family dwellings. These may be palatial if the family is particularly wealthy. These houses are

Camel racing is popular amongst the Emiratis and the trade in racing camels is a source of income for those who maintain a Bedouin lifestyle.

often built around a courtyard so all rooms open into the central garden. The grounds are enclosed by high walls and a gate making the once open tent-home of the desert a socially impenetrable fortress. However, the outer wall does serve the more positive purpose of providing protection from the desert for the inner garden to grow. Within the walls, some rooms are built as separate structures. The floors of the rooms are covered with Persian carpets, walls and ceilings are completely wallpapered and there are pillows to sit on. There are chests, bookcases or low tables in some rooms but furniture in a Western sense still does not feature prominently in their homes.

Conspicuous Wealth

Their houses are equipped with electricity and running water. There may be several televisions, refrigerators, cookers (ovens), and washing machines in each house. Many of the Emiratis are wealthy to an astounding extent. Some own dozens of cars, wear Rolex watches, hire an army of servants, have a palace in their hometown and also one in the vacation resort of Al-Ain or another poorer Arab country (Syria

An Emirati man talking on a mobile phone beside his shiny 4WD.

for example). When a family member becomes seriously ill, that person may be flown to a hospital in London in a private lear jet to receive the best medical care money can buy. The family travels along and is catered to by the London staff.

The Emiratis can be annoying with their wealth. For example, most Emirati men carry portable telephones. The Emiratis, by the way, have very up to date communication systems, again, the best money can buy. Many of them don't have important enough business to warrant the need for a phone at all times but an Emiratis' purpose in communicating is often to establish, confirm and reaffirm relationships; "Hello, how are you, how is your health, how is your mother, father, and everyone else in your family?" is considered very purposeful communication to them.

Young men attending the university, leave their 4WD vehicles running so the air conditioner can keep the truck cool while they attend their two hour English class. Midway through the first hour their friend calls just to say hello. The Western male teacher tries to conduct class over the din of ringing telephones and students going and coming from the hall where they talk to the caller. The students respond to the teacher's frustration with, "No problem, Sir." But it is a problem and a huge source of frustration for the teacher, who places great importance on what he is doing and the time given him to accomplish his task. The conflict is with a time orientation, where the teacher has a plan for tomorrow and the day after tomorrow all eventually culminating in the successful completion of the course. The Emiratis are not future oriented and are comfortable with learning or doing tomorrow whatever didn't get accomplished today.

Work Ethic

Westerners often view the Emiratis as decadent and spoiled and have a whole host of negative feelings arising from a lack of understanding. It is said that Arabs are adverse to physical labour, particularly if it dirties their hands or makes them sweat. The Emiratis do not work with their hands (perhaps with the exception of the women as mentioned above). They view doing projects around the house as demeaning and think our hobbies and pride in completed projects is quaint.

Indoor labour is preferable to outdoor labour and office work, such as clerk, secretary, or postal worker is better yet. Their work ethic is unlike that of the Protestant work ethic prevalent in the West. They avoid work that requires the use of muscles, do not engage in agricultural work except in research and management positions and do not make handicrafts. Some Emiratis see work as a curse and hold the acquisition of wealth through luck as the ideal. However, gambling is illegal (against Islam). While they do not believe in gambling, opportunities abound to win large cash prizes or cars from businesses trying to increase their numbers of customers.

Earning favour in the eyes of someone important in order to advance one's work position is also positively valued. So, nepotism is prevalent among them and the legion of foreigners are there to do their labour. Westerners ridicule them for their 'hypocrisy' and nepotism, non-Gulf Arabs envy them, but the Emiratis themselves believe they are blessed by Allah and have their just rewards as predetermined by Him. However, even understanding this may not help you to excuse some of what you will see.

The further away from manual labour Emiratis get, the higher their status. In a country as wealthy as the Emirates and where the wealth is controlled by less than a quarter of the population, the Emiratis never have to dirty their hands. Many of them are owners of businesses and real estate (only a national may purchase land). These owners, called businessmen, may also hold government positions from policeman to ruler. While having kept some of the values of the past and integrating them into a changed lifestyle, the modern Emiratis have insulated themselves from the rest of the population by high walls, tinted windows and special privileges.

We might view the Emirati who chooses to continue the desert life as poor and the city dweller as rich. However, the Bedouin way of life is highly revered and even the city dweller lives by the values and beliefs of the Bedouin. Not all Emiratis are wealthy, have good family connections or have traditions that are highly revered. Poor Emiratis are most likely to be encountered in the northern, less wealthy emirates. They make their living from fishing, shop keeping, and trading. The well educated among them work as teachers and researchers. Abu Dhabi provides the northern emirates with funds for an infrastructure, so education and health care are provided. While these Emiratis are less likely to live in palaces, their needs are met.

Manners

You should always be polite with the Emiratis. Most of them treat expatriates very well. If you anger them (thankfully this is difficult to do) there can be repercussions, especially if the Emirati is highly placed. The young Emirati men can be annoying. Some of them are full of their own status yet lack the grace to treat others with dignity. They hoot and holler at women from their car windows, push ahead in lines, park their cars anywhere they please (for example, behind your parked car at the supermarket), and generally behave like young men in most countries. Most of their less desirable behaviour occurs when they are in their 4WDs, mercedes and BMWs as though their vehicles give them license to forget the values they were taught. If possible, say *haram* (meaning forbidden) and the rules they learned in the majlis should kick in and change their poor manners. The government is attempting to curtail poor behaviour by arresting the offenders and publishing their pictures in the newspapers in order to embarrass them into behaving properly.

Emiratis are very comfortable with life in the Emirates. Not surprisingly, it suits them better than any other group. You will only see the women from afar, they may smile at you when you are both in line at the grocery store, otherwise you will not see them. You will have some contact with the men at government offices, in some small businesses, and in brief encounters in daily life. These encounters can be pleasant or unpleasant depending on your willingness to under-stand them on their terms and not your own. If you take their actions and behaviour from an educated, open-minded perspective, you are more likely to view an interruption as an opportunity to observe them and learn and your patience will be rewarded with a glimpse into a culture marked by politeness, generosity and respect. Otherwise the lack of line formation, the honking horns and the flaunted wealth and status are going to stand out for you. The Middle East and most other parts of the world are opposite in so many ways that life in the Emirates lends itself to constant conflict.

NON GULF ARABS – SEVEN TRADES BUT NO LUCK

The non-Gulf Arabs tend to be well educated. However, they do not command much respect. Gulf Arabs and non-Gulf Arabs do not like each other. The non-Gulf Arabs view the 'Gulfies' as little better than tribes with flags. At the same time, they are envious of the Emiratis' wealth. Gulf Arabs tend to look down their noses at their overpopu-lated, poverty-stricken neighbours who can't seem to solve their political problems.

Non-Gulf Arabs are often fluent in English and French as well as Arabic, as these languages are widely spoken in their home countries. Speaking these languages is a mark of considerable education. They are also a highly skilled group. Many of them have their own businesses in the UAE which they may own outright if they began those businesses long enough ago. Nowadays an Emirati must own 51% of a business. Still other members of this group are professors at the university, doctors, or some other type of professional. They are paid considerably less than their Western counterparts and are shown considerably less respect as well.

Non-Gulf Arabs are as family oriented as the Emiratis are. Friends and spouses are usually met or made through family connections and socialising tends to be in the home at large family gatherings. This is not possible for them in the Emirates where only their nuclear family is present. As a result, this group may feel quite isolated. There is no real structure to replace their familiar method of socialising either. The Emirates can be a lonely, isolated place for members of this group.

Some of these Arabs are Muslim and some are Christian. The men wear Western dress so it is difficult to determine their religious persuasion. The women also wear Western dress, though it is very conservative – long skirts, high necklines, and full length sleeves. However, they do cover their heads if they are Muslim. In their own countries they may have discarded the tradition of always covering their heads but they feel pressured to do so in the Emirates. Their head scarves are different from the Emiratis' in that they are white or multicoloured and multi-patterned instead of black. If you pay close attention, you can even distinguish differences in the way the head scarf is worn.

Christian Arab men often mingle with the Westerners. They must be careful of situations where there is alcohol and they could stand the chance of being mistaken for a Muslim by virtue of their nationality. Some I have run into at social gatherings have admitted nervousness for this reason. Many of the non-Gulf Arab men come to the Emirates without their families. They choose to work in the Emirates for 8 to 10 months each year and spend their vacation at home with their families.

Contact with this group can take many forms. Some of them resent the privileges and respect given you, especially as many of them are far more educated and experienced. Attempts to be friendly may be useless and you will want to avoid contact with them. Others like most everything about you and are warm, open and friendly. Of course, the same rules usually apply when dealing with them as outlined above with the Emiratis – women with women and men with men. Perhaps the best advice is to be polite and respectful to members of this group and learn about them in order to know how not to offend them. You are very likely to have contact with them since they are likely to be working in the same field as you.

LABOURERS

Labourers are the largest group of people in the Emirates. They come from Pakistan, Afghanistan, India, and other Asian subcontinent countries. They are lumped together in this telling according to your likely contact with them. You usually don't have or shouldn't have direct contact with them. They clean the streets, water the fields, tend the animals, and hire themselves out. Many of them are illegal immigrants and must take what work they can get. For the most part the illegal aliens are tolerated, but when the political atmosphere between the Arab world and the Asian subcontinent becomes tense or when a labourer commits a serious crime, illegal immigrants are rounded up and shipped home.

The labourers are all men. They do not earn enough money to support their families in this country. However, they do make three or four times as much in the Emirates as they could in their own countries. They live in squalid conditions, as many as 12 men may share one room. They pool their resources to prepare their evening meal and they send their earnings home. They live like this for years, often until they are old men. They can then go home and enjoy the 'fruits of their labour' among the children and grandchildren they have sired on their few vacations home.

These men speak Hindi or Urdu and often Arabic as well. They usually do not speak English. Better jobs among this group are taxi driver, fisherman, or shopkeeper. Those men who do speak English have higher earnings and a better standard of living.

These men are unaccustomed to seeing Westerners. Their impression of women is taken from movies and is not favourable. There is little you can do to educate them or change their belief. They will stare at you. Women should not make eye contact with them and certainly should not speak to them. Eye contact is taken as an invitation. It is

Foreign labourers live in makeshift accommodation but make more money than they could earn in their own countries.

unfortunate to have to go around constantly averting your eyes, and in this respect the Emirati women are fortunate to have their heads covered. They can see out but people cannot see in. They are free to look about them. So are you, of course, but you may have to then fend off a lot of unwanted attention.

Highly educated subcontinent citizens have jobs requiring skill and education. Their earnings are high and they usually have their families with them. They may even have established several generations of family in the Emirates. They command respect, mix well with Westerners and retain many of their values. Examples of this are to continue a tradition of arranged marriages (much in keeping with the host culture) and to educate children according to the standards of the home country, even if it means sending them abroad to study.

WESTERNERS

The majority of Westerners in the UAE come from England. Others come from The United States, Australia, New Zealand, Scotland, Canada, and Africa. A few come from non English speaking countries in Europe. Some enjoy the lifestyle, the weather and the generous salaries so much, they establish several generations of family, making the Emirates their new home. They teach English, staff hospitals, run and maintain oil rigs, work in the import/export field, provide professional services from counselling to massage, and provide training of all kinds. In other words, they work in occupations that require special skill, training, or education and a fluent, native-like command of English.

They tend to be well paid with housing and expenses paid for by their companies. They work reasonable hours and have at least a month of vacation time each year, usually more. They have an abundance of leisure time and they fill it in clever, boredom alleviating ways. This is the group you will probably have the most contact with. While there is much mixing among nationalities, birds of a feather still flock together.

Chapter Three

COPING WITH CULTURE SHOCK

Things are not good and not bad, they are just different
—Author's mantra

WHAT IS CULTURE SHOCK?

Culture shock is what afflicts people who spend prolonged periods of time in another country. It pertains to how people cope with the stress caused by the newness of the environment, culture, and people. The stress can feel like an illness and can cause physical problems such as allergies, backaches and headaches or interrupt the normal digestive processes. It can bring on emotional stress expressed through unexpected and inexplicable tears or vehemently expressed anger over minor offences. It can also unsettle a person intellectually to the point where they don't know who to trust and can't distinguish between reality and the fabrications of their imagination. People who are already under some emotional stress will feel the effects of culture shock much more severely than those who are not.

Does it happen to everybody? Yes, to one degree or another. Even people who have experienced it before must go through it again in a new country and culture. You can hardly even be aware of the stress and changes you've been through until you watch other newcomers go through it and remember your own similar experience and feelings in the situations and how much more comfortable you feel with the passage of time. Does knowing what to expect help or even prevent culture shock? It helps some, but it can't prevent it. Is culture shock realised in single, isolated events? No. It is a stage of development one goes through in adapting to a new culture. It does not begin or end at specific times, nor is it brought on by individual and isolated incidents. It may recur in smaller doses throughout your stay.

Three Stages

In adapting to a new culture, one goes through about three stages. An individual enters and exits these stages repeatedly but tends to fall within one of the three at any given time. The initial stage is one of euphoria in which everything about the culture and the overseas experience is new and wonderful. The newcomer presents a rather naive self at this point. They then progress to the shock stage in which they are extremely angry and negative about the host culture and country. The final stage is one of acceptance. The developing newcomer realises that life in the new country is different from what was familiar to them and learns to operate comfortably within those differences. This third stage is not a permanent one, not in the Emirates. Each stage must be worked through again and again with each new culture one comes into contact with and even repeatedly with a culture one has been in contact with.

Why does culture shock happen? It happens because people expect others to behave, think and feel as they do. Newcomers to a culture experience a constant barrage of conflicting behaviours. They are making sense of their daily lives according to the way their home culture organised life. When they must act or react in situations in the new culture, they will do so according to the rules of their own, at least until they learn new ways of behaving. Their behaviour may not be appropriate in the new environment causing them to be misunderstood, cause offence, or be caused offence.

Newly arrived expatriates must learn the new ways of behaving and change some of their behaviours, thoughts, and emotions in order to cope in the new environment. Frequent encounters resulting in misunderstandings cause newcomers to feel anxious, confused, irritated and helpless. They may experience moments of depression and choose to withdraw from the world around them. They may feel extremely homesick and find themselves writing endless letters home. They may join other expatriates in drowning their feelings in alcohol and making disparaging remarks about the host culture. They may even develop paranoid thinking that people are watching every move they make.

THE INITIAL SHOCK

Each person arrives in the Emirates with their own special set of expectations. As these are not met, the newcomer becomes intolerant and expresses annoyance in little outbursts of rage. Such phrases as, "This would never happen in my home country," "These people are so backward, why can't they get it right?" and "Arabs are crazy!" dominate the conversation of the culture shock sufferer. The frustrations which arise when your methods of coping with problems aren't working cause you more stress than you realise. The more you insist on your view and your way and the less tolerance you have in a situation, the more frustrating it will be for you.

One of the frustrating situations you will encounter initially is trying to make your way from home to work. You will be cut off by other drivers or the car next to you may slow down and speed up so the driver can keep pace and leer at you. You will find yourself waiting endless hours for deliveries that are never made. You will be in a rush and try to pick something up at a store only to find the shop keeper hasn't managed to make it back from prayer yet. You buy something at a store and are told by every other person you mention it to that they found it somewhere else for less. Sometimes you find you've paid far too much and become angry that you are feeding three generations of a family in India with your generosity.

There are many other possibilities for situations that may be frustrating for you. Anger, outrage, and frustration are normal reactions. However, the Emiratis are outwardly gentle people who believe it is shameful to show rage. People around you will be amazed and embarrassed if you lose your temper. Aim for humour to diffuse the tension or take a few deep breaths.

CULTURE SHOCK UAE

Descriptions of culture shock assume it is one culture you are adjusting to. The Emirates are unique in that a single culture to adjust and settle in to does not exist. It would appear that one has many choices of culture with which to mix. This too is a myth. Choices are severely restricted by gender, language and social status. Outside of the expatriate group, men and women do not mix socially at any level. It is against the rules and norms of the society. Language can also be a limitation. English and Arabic are widely spoken but there are many who only speak Urdu or Hindi (or German or Italian!). If you choose to flout class boundaries and make a friend with a labourer who does have a reasonable command of English, he will probably misunderstand your overtures, make erroneous assumptions about you and your motives, and behave in ways likely to cause you offence.

When living overseas, you may be given advice to avoid the expatriate community and mix with the locals. You don't have the luxury of making a choice in the Emirates. The expatriate community is impossible to escape. On the streets you are as likely to see an

Emirati as you are a Westerner and you are more likely to see Westerners than Emiratis at work, at the beach or at shopping malls. The Emiratis you do meet may be unwilling to form a friendship with you because of past bad experiences or because the Koran advises against making friends with Jews or Christians. You may have to persevere long and hard to form a friendship. Your efforts will be worth it because Emiratis take friendship very seriously and friendships with them are life long endeavours to work at and to be cherished.

Your chances of mixing with the Emiratis would be easier if you found work outside one of the major cities, in a village in one of the northern emirates. Contact with them is on their terms and close friendships must be earned. They may also try very hard to understand you but foreign ways are very strange to them.

During the honeymoon stage you will find the sand dunes are beautiful; the parties are fun; the Arab women, hidden behind their veils, are mysterious; and the markets hum with life and delicious smells. About four to six months after you arrive, the sand dunes all look the same as those you keep sweeping out from under the beds and corners of the rooms. The same people are at all the parties you attend, complaining about the same things. The mysterious women have been relegated, in your opinion, to women without the backbone to stand up for their independence. Constantly negotiating prices with people is more trouble than it's worth so you are sticking to the few expensive stores that are 'honest' enough to mark their products.

You've experienced enough to begin making decisions about the kind of life you want here. It is time to choose the kinds of friends and kinds of experiences you want to have. Positive, upbeat friends will keep you from withdrawing. You need same gender friends to give you respectability and to help you weather the inevitable gossip. This same gender group may also be your reality anchor, much as a family is for its members.

Expat behaviours may seem somewhat familiar to you. Most everyone speaks English fluently. They like the same familiar activities, use the same modern conveniences and products, and they have similar tastes in dress, music, etc. They are from many different cultures though, each making sense of and organising life according to a different set of rules. The most obvious difference is linguistic. Each group uses slightly different vocabulary and speaks with a slightly different accent. These differences form the basis of many interesting and humorous discussions.

Most Western newcomers stick to what is available and familiar – other Westerners. This requires its own adjustment. There are differences among the Westerners that are not so obvious. The independent American soon tires of her Spanish friend's constant presence. The distant Brit is offended by his Egyptian friend's inquisitive, personal questions. The Australian is surprised to find her male friends have ulterior motives beyond simple straightforward friendship. The Scotsman becomes fed up with having to continually adjust his accent to be comprehensible to other native English speakers. Most everyone grows tired of being ridiculed for every stereotype particular to their country. They find themselves alternately representing and defending their home country. Laughter is a good antidote. So is education. Even altering one person's misconceptions or generalisations of your culture can feel rewarding. The best advice is to not make generalisations. Watch, listen and learn about the people around you.

With a constant variety of cultural contact, it is impossible to adjust and settle in to one culture. Thus, people form friendships with those they have most in common with. These are people from their home country, people they work with, people in the same profession, or team-mates from the sport they are participating in.

GOSSIP

Gossip is rampant. It goes hand in hand with boredom. You will find yourself the focus of gossip from time to time with or without cause. Stories are sometimes embellished. In the face of so many ways of acting, ways of thinking and ways of feeling, rules and boundaries vary and the truth can be pretty amazing on its own. Ignore the gossip and fight the boredom by engaging in activities that teach you something new.

The more you can learn about the Emiratis, the more interesting life will be for you. This may involve learning how to apply henna, learning how to belly dance, or learning about the archeology and geology of the country. Or it may involve passing long, quiet hours in the company of an Emirati as he or she grows comfortable enough to accept you.

THE SHORT TIMER'S ATTITUDE

People who have decided to leave the Emirates sometimes develop a short timer's attitude, even if their leave date is six months or more away. They stop making friends and begin to distance themselves from the people and activities around them. A few people have this attitude from the beginning of their stay and keep it no matter how many years they remain in the Emirates. These people can be particularly negative about their environment in an effort to cope with and maintain their transient state. Perhaps this is their particular reaction to culture shock.

SINGLES/MARRIEDS

The Emirates, Dubai in particular, are a Gulf playground. 'Swinging single' Westerners from their late teens through their thirties abound. They seem to be having a wonderful time bouncing from one party to the next, but are they? Living in a Club Med like atmosphere eventually grows old and boredom takes hold.

Married people and people with families have responsibilities to each other. These responsibilities give their lives structure and they are able to support each other. Couples can face their difficulties together with someone they love and trust while single people don't readily have this luxury. An added bonus for married women is that

Many expats enjoy social occasions such as the Dubai Cup.

they have an ever present male escort to shelter them from some of the hardships single women face. However, the marriage bears the stress of living overseas. Couples either grow closer together or further apart. Married people too frequently make the mistake of thinking the singles' lives are so much more interesting and exciting than their dull stay-at-home existence.

Wives who do not work (and more frequently of late, husbands) are at home and alone too much. There is not a ready built social support system for them and no welcoming neighbour to ease their arrival. The maid does the housework and the boredom becomes unbearable. Couples need to be aware of the extra stress before they arrive in order to decide together how best to cope with it. Making friends and spending time with other couples while avoiding the singles scene is advisable.

BEFORE YOU ARRIVE

Your excitement about coming to the Emirates may well be dampened by the fears and generalisations your family and co-workers may relay to you. There is nothing to fear. Life in the Emirates will settle into as much of a routine as life in your home country. It will be a different routine, but it will be routine nonetheless.

One major stereotype you may encounter is that Arabs are hypocritical, professing belief in one thing and acting in a diametrically opposed manner. While it is true in reality that some Arabs are hypocritical, looked at from the perspective of their values and beliefs, their socially acceptable behaviour makes sense and is not hypocritical. Much of the scholarly work you will find on the Arabs has been written by Westerners and usually paints an unflattering picture of them. This indicates an unwillingness or an inability to take the Arabic perspective.

ADVICE FOR COPING

Adjusting will be facilitated by reading about the Emiratis and building interest in them and their country. Also, knowing the cultural meanings behind your daily frustrations will cause them to be less frustrating. Neighbouring Oman offers you endless hours of exploration of yet another culture if the one you are in simply never opens up to you. It is a beautiful place to travel in, too.

See yourself as being fortunate to live in a place where you can learn about so many different people. View your friendships as permanent and count yourself fortunate to know people from many countries. Learn a little Arabic. You are not expected to know much or do well with it, but Arabs will be flattered that you tried. It is not difficult to learn a dozen or so very useful phrases either (see Chapter Eight).

Focus on positive aspects of the environment and spend time with other positively focused people. Finally, lower your expectations of yourself and others. Allow more time to accomplish errands or to complete projects, especially in the beginning when you are adjusting. Whether you realise it or not, you are under additional stress and you constantly need to take care of yourself.

— Chapter Four —

MARRIAGE AND FAMILY

EXTENDED FAMILIES

Emiratis value family highly. They usually have large families of from 7 to 13 or more members. Emirati families consist of one husband, one or two wives, and numerous children. However, the concept of family extends well beyond the Western concept of a nucleus, to include extended members as well – aunts, uncles, grandparents and cousins many times removed. Emiratis feel a strong alliance to all these kin and loyalty to family members takes precedence over other loyalties or responsibilities. Loyalties are so strong that family obligations may absent an Emirati from work or school. This is beyond the Emirati's control. You will probably only be informed of a student's or workmate's absence after the fact, since speaking of it beforehand may constitute prediction and a control over the future that the Emirati does not have.

52

ROLE OF THE FATHER

The father is the head of the family nucleus. Emiratis believe in paternal rule, at least in public. The father is responsible for making sure the members of his family subordinate their personal interests to those of the group and to those of the father as representative of the smaller family group. A man's status and authority increase through age, experience, and cleverness and his advice is sought from kin who are less established financially or socially. He is an authoritarian in public, albeit a gentle one, while his rule in private might be less dictatorial.

The father is not only responsible for his wife and children but also for his parents and any unmarried sisters he has. He must provide for their welfare and in the case of the women, protect their virtue. At home he is responsible for meting out punishment. Punishment is usually gentle in nature as long as the 'crime' has not brought shame or dishonour upon the family. However, he may be merciless if the crime has brought shame. A wife or daughter engaging in illicit sex would incur the greatest possible shame on the family.

The father loves his children but does not openly show it. He should have many children to prove his virility and may take more than one wife in order to procure these. Muslims are permitted to marry up to four wives as long as they provide equally for each wife and treat each wife as fairly and generously as the others. Wives are kept in separate chambers and are not typically friendly to each other as they are in competition for the attention of their mutual husband and are vying for power through the production and governance of the most children, preferably male ones.

Having two or more wives was typical of the previous generations but is becoming less common because it is difficult to provide equally for so many and also difficult to keep peace in the house. The difficulty in keeping more than one wife has increased with the acquisition of wealth. Wives now require more in the way of goods and services and the husband is often away on business and therefore

53

Emirati father and son – the father is the head of the family and his status increases with age. Sons are valued as potential protectors of the group.

less available to give enough attention to one wife, let alone two. Further, both the Koran and the Prophet Mohammed encouraged having only one wife even though more were allowed. Many Emiratis are confused by the question, "How many brothers and sisters do you have?" because they don't know if you are asking the total their mother has borne or the total their father has sired. It is becoming increasingly rare for a man to take more than one wife and most men today do not have more than one or two wives. Also, a woman or her parents can insist that a stipulation preventing marriage to any more wives be written into a marriage contract or *mut'a*.

ROLE OF THE MOTHER

> In the eye of its mother, a monkey is a gazelle.
>
> —UAE proverb

Mothers are primarily occupied in providing their children with emotional support. There are virtually no employment opportunities for the Emirati woman, her life is her family. Thus, she puts great effort into making herself her children's sole emotional support in an effort to keep her children dependent on her. Their dependence is important to her because the only power an Emirati woman wields is through her children. The more children she has, the greater are her power and status.

As with men, a woman's status increases with age. Her opinion is sought increasingly as she ages and as a grandmother, she is a common source of advice in both personal and business matters. Women spend their days visiting close neighbours and members of their family or shopping. Nowadays there are opportunities for the older generation of women to gain some education as adult literacy classes are being provided by the government for those who grew up before education existed in their country.

A patient and loving mother is an admirable one, so a mother is inclined to spoil her children, boys in particular, who will grow up to provide for her and protect her. Although traditionally the more children a woman had the greater her status, these days women are getting married later in life and having fewer children. This is a result of Western influence, where child brides are not acceptable and higher education is necessary. While there are numerous adults around influencing children, mothers are still the greatest influence in their lives.

Education and Employment

Emirati women are attempting to graduate from university and even be employed prior to marrying. The operative word is 'attempting' because few attain these goals, particularly not the latter. While a young woman is attending university, her parents may be approached with an offer for their daughter. The family may put pressure on the daughter to accept. Once she does, power and responsibility over the direction her life will take passes from her father to her husband. Responsibilities of being a wife, and soon a mother, may prevent a woman from pursuing her education further and employment is out of the question. Her husband may not want her to be educated any further and can prevent her attending university. He probably would not want his wife to work.

A mother faces divorce if she does not produce children. It is assumed the physical failing is hers and she is sent back to her family in disgrace. Children bring men prestige and women a solid marriage. A woman feels she disappoints her husband if she doesn't produce children, particularly a son. The union of marriage is based on gaining financial status for the woman and social status for the man. Romance often grows and is certainly hoped for. Procreation is a necessary and expected outcome.

ROLE OF CHILDREN

It is said that a child's heart is like a precious jewel without inscription; it is therefore ready to absorb whatever is engraved upon it. Children are expected to be utterly respectful of elders. They are frequently in the company of adults, interacting with them and being disciplined by them – all of them. This they accept from all elders.

Because they are so much in contact with older relatives, they are influenced by them and learn social values of the Bedouin, such as hospitality. They learn well and can serve you competently. They also learn utter loyalty to the group. Thus, the values of the group are accepted without question. They are not kept apart from adults as something not yet 'done,' they are integrated. Children are taught to believe in paternal rule. They love, respect and also fear their fathers while they are emotionally attached to their mothers.

Children are not always given a bed time, especially during school breaks. They play until all hours of the night, until they are tired enough to go to sleep on their own or until everyone else also goes to sleep. This can be annoying for people who must be up and at work by 8:00 a.m. – earplugs might be a wise investment! Emiratis are in general very flexible in the hours they keep and have a more relaxed attitude towards time.

Children attend school six days a week. In addition to regular subjects, they study the Arabic language and English through rote memorisation. Some parents send their children to private schools but most still have a relaxed attitude towards education. Children do not have responsibilities outside the classroom, rather they are given the freedom to play in a safe and secure environment.

The Difference Between Girls and Boys

Female children, *banat*, are valued for their potential son-producing abilities. Male children, *awlad*, for their ability to protect the group. Since male children were of use to the group in their early teens for protecting the group and providing food and the female children could only produce the next generation which then had to grow up before they were of use, it was preferable to sire male children. This preference has survived in the present, even when physical protection of the group has ceased to be a daily concern.

Girls are taught to be subservient early in their development and are less likely to require discipline than boys. Boys and girls are provided different role models. Fathers and older brothers come and go as they please. Their needs are satisfied on demand by servants or female family members. Little boys see this and learn to be aggressive and decisive. They begin by demanding their mother's breast which is still given to the age of two. Boys learn to expect similar relationships with women thereafter, believing women are there to serve and obey.

Girls reflect subservience and passivity in their behaviour. They are made to relinquish their toys to a brother when he demands them. They are kept at home with the other women and small children. They do not have the freedom to come and go as the boys and men do. This is slowly changing in the large cities. Young women are meeting each other for coffee in public coffee shops. Many Emiratis are appalled by such 'brazen' behaviour, others are ready to accept the change. A few centres have been built exclusively for women for them to meet and socialise. No doubt more of these will be established to allow women greater freedom without sacrificing social mores.

Emiratis did not go through an adolescent stage in the past. As soon as they reached puberty they were accepted as adults, eligible for marriage and expected to help protect and provide for the family. Young women could be married after their first menstruation and have children while they were not yet grown themselves. This is changing with education, albeit slowly. It is more common now for young men and women to attend university before they marry. As education affects the social mores, the adolescent stage is becoming more apparent. Freedom and curiosity are having their effect and when these adolescents do marry and have children, it is likely there will be even bigger changes with the next generation.

PARENTAL INFLUENCE

Parental influence never ceases in a person's life. Emiratis live at home until they are married. The couple then live with the husband's parents. Nowadays some couples occasionally live on their own in housing provided by their parents. A divorced woman will return automatically to her parents' home. Blood ties are stronger than marriage ties and children will turn to the family home for advice rather than to their spouse. The older generation is respected more as they age. Their lifetime of experience provides a source of wisdom that is consulted by younger generations and they govern the family as the matriarch or patriarch until their death.

TRIBAL MENTALITY

To a tribe the individual is unimportant. All words and actions take the group into consideration. Emiratis were economically motivated to marry members of their own group and motivated to increase the group numbers to enhance survival opportunities. It is still desirable to keep the money in the family and marriages among first cousins are encouraged, even though the Emiratis have been educated about the increased risk of birth defects among babies born of parents whose blood is too closely related. They have evidence of this among themselves. Crossed-eyes are the most commonly seen defect. Less commonly seen defects are missing limbs, limbs of unequal length, or limbs of a disproportionate size to the rest of the body. Emiratis with more serious defects such as mental instability or who are grossly deformed are kept locked away from society at home or in hospital wards.

Protecting the Group

Group survival remains a modern day concern. However, the danger affecting group survival is no longer the physical environment. Rather, group survival is being affected by the acceptance of Western values. Young men study in the West and meet and sometimes marry Western women. Marriages outside their culture afford them greater social freedoms such as dining in mixed company. Emirati men marry outside their culture against their parents wishes and even the government is involved in actively discouraging out-group marriages. An Emirati man who marries an Emirati woman is awarded dh70,000 by the government (about US$20,000). He is not eligible for this bonus if he marries outside the group.

The group protect themselves in other ways. For example, they wear their national dress when in the country and discourage foreigners from wearing it. They are easily distinguishable from afar. Within the country, men and women are educated but that education is as devoid as possible of any but the Emirati and Muslim cultural and religious knowledge. The party line is very much presented and accepted. Ask 100 Emiratis under the age of 20 the same questions and you will get the same answers 100 times. Neither Islam nor the tribe allow for questioning of what is presented as the truth.

SEGREGATION

Emiratis believe people cannot resist sexual temptation. A man and a woman alone in a room will have intercourse, it is a foregone conclusion. Women are helpless and cannot resist. Men know this. To protect their reputations, strict segregation is practised amongst the Emiratis. As Western values and practices are more and more visible everywhere, the practice becomes stricter. Women are only ever in the company of other women or else they are being accompanied somewhere by a brother, father, or husband. Emirati women must protect their reputation because its loss will ruin their marriage chances. There are few opportunities for women outside of marriage. Womens' reputations can be lost if they appear loose. Looseness might include being unescorted in public, not covering their faces, or any number of surprising subtleties.

These beliefs and practices affect the expatriate population. Unescorted women are shocking to the Emiratis and to the large labour population, many of whom also believe women should always be covered and escorted. When a man sees a woman by herself, he is shocked. The constant everyday focus on women as taboo of course sets them up as objects to be pursued. Those most likely to be pursued are those who are seen as most accessible – Western women. Since it is assumed women cannot resist temptation, 'No!' comes as quite a shock to the pursuant.

SLAVERY

Sharia law states that slaves must be treated with justice and kindness. It also states that while slavery is acceptable, a Muslim cannot be enslaved. The Emiratis kept slaves until the British forced them to stop this practice. Prior to British intervention, slaves were captured in war, were bought, or were born into their position. They were often trusted companions, raised to their work and taught tribal values. Slaves were often as loyal to the group as the master was. The relationship between a master and his trusted slave could be so close

that the slave would conduct the master's business and marry the master's daughter when he had been granted his freedom.

Now that the system is gone, paid foreigners fill the slaves' shoes but without the trust and relationship of the past. Emiratis prefer having Muslim servants in their homes. These servants are found in surprising places: India, Malaysia, Thailand, and other countries that still have Muslim communities left from the days when the Islamic Empire was at its greatest command. Poor families will send their daughters and sons to the Gulf to work, who then send their earnings home to support the family.

THE HAREM

The word *harem* conjures up images of a roomful of beautiful young women lounging about waiting to attend to the needs of the master. It is a somewhat exaggerated image. The harem refers to the group of women of a household. Within this group are the wife (or wives), the husband's mother, the daughters, the young children, the female servants, and any visiting female guests. Since women are kept so secluded the word harem has changed from meaning women to meaning forbidden. It is pronounced 'ha-RAM,' with the stress on the second syllable, and is now used in a wider context for anything that is against Islam.

NAMES AND TITLES

Emiratis are given a first name taken from the Koran or a paternal grandparent. The first name is followed by their father's name, then by their paternal grandfather's name (so a boy named after his grandfather will have the same first and third names – Abdulla Ali Abdulla, for example), then by their paternal great grandfather's name and so forth, all the way back to the Prophet Mohammed. Thus, a person's name reveals their paternal genealogy. Even women who have a female first name, have a string of male names following their first name. When a woman marries, she keeps her father's name rather than taking her husband's because she always belongs to her father.

A person's name also denotes the tribe he or she belongs to but where in the name the tribe is represented is inconsistent. This inconsistency can create confusion in payroll, billing systems, and the telephone book, all of which opt for using a different system of alphabetising. One will alphabetise by first name, another by father's name and yet another by the grandfather's name.

People are addressed as Mr., Mrs., Miss, or a title (if they have one) as a sign of respect, plus their first name. The rest of the names are usually dropped, unless two Ali's or two Fatima's need to frequently be distinguished from each other.

There are some special titles for special cases. Sheikh is used to address or refer to a tribal leader or his sons and Sheikha is used to address his wife. Children might be called by their first name + *bin* or *ibu* (son of) or *bint* (daughter of) + father's name (for example, Ali bin Shakbut or Fatima bint Nuaimi).

When couples have a son, the name they are addressed by changes to *abu* (father of) or *amm* (mother of) + the name of the child. For example, when Mohammed Ali Saeed has a son he names Ali Mohammed Ali (given name + father's name + grandfather's name), Mohammed is addressed as abu Ali (father of Ali) and his wife is amm Ali. These forms of address are informal and are used by friends and family as a sign of respect and recognition of the couple's good fortune.

People are addressed by their first names because it is the only one of their names that is theirs alone. Most names have meaning. Examples of female names are Fatima (nursed at her mother's breast), Ibtesam (smile), Jameela (beautiful) and Amal (hope). Examples of male names are Aziz (dear), Hassan (good), Amir (prince) and Hamad (praise). Names frequently given to children are taken from famous people in Islamic history such as Mohammed and Fatima. If an Arab has a Christian sounding name such as George or Robert, he is probably a Christian.

MARRIAGE

Marriage is not idealised. While love and companionship are important, so are financial security, social status, and children. The goal of marriage is to have a happy and harmonious life together. Marriages are usually stable and partners are respectful to each other. Marriages are arranged. Parents choose potential partners for their children. These choices are made based on reputation. Men should have good social and financial standing and women should be both beautiful and virtuous.

Since a person's reputation is so fundamental to making a good match, women are always escorted in public or covered in mixed company and a man is not frivolous in his interactions with others or with his money. Since there are so few Emiratis, everyone knows everyone else or at least knows of them, their reputation and their eligibility. It is important for an Emirati to marry someone of equal or higher status. Parents wish to find a compatible, genial match for their children so they may have happy lives together. If love also grows, it is all the better.

Making an Offer

A young Emirati man may receive suggestions from his parents, relatives and friends as to whom he should marry. People will report to him on their sister's beauty and virtue. They may even show him

63

a picture if one can be obtained. The father of the young man then approaches the parents of the woman who has been chosen and makes an offer for her. The woman's parents learn what they can about the suitor's reputation and prospects. If he is acceptable, the parents relay his offer to their daughter. She may accept or refuse the suitor. Parents greatly affect their daughter's decision in how they present the offer.

The degree to which women are consulted on their choice of husband varies from family to family. Some fathers allow their daughters accompanied time to meet and interview their suitors. The young couple are shy together, it possibly being their first time in the company of the opposite sex who is not an immediate family member. Daughters enquire as to how they will be kept, what opportunities they will be allowed to study and work, where they will live, how many wives the husband intends to take, and how much they will be able to see their families after joining their in-laws' household. Potential brides and grooms must trust their parents advice and wisdom to gain such knowledge or trust the gossip they hear from other female relatives to determine the other's suitability.

A young person who marries without parental consent is expelled from the family and hence from the tribe. In the past, expulsion resulted in death in the desert. Parental wishes were almost always obeyed and rebellion remains uncommon today. Parents cannot force a girl to marry against her will, but a young woman has to be careful in turning down offers because another might not come along and she does not want to remain single, since her only opportunity for power in life is as a matriarch of a family. A young woman brings wealth to her family in marrying and she knows her value in that sense. Fathers can and some do marry their young daughters off to decaying, old men. When the old husband dies, the daughter is married to another old man. In this way, the father can keep collecting huge dowries. This practice is not socially acceptable and such a father brings shame to himself and his family.

Finding a Spouse

Marriage is arranged Victorian style by the parents in a very meaning-ful and carefully planned manner. Marriage is the event with the greatest importance in an Emirati's life. Marriage to a cousin is preferred and marriage to a first cousin is considered to be the best possible match. The families know each other and the bride and groom would have met as children. Emiratis believe these marriages have a greater chance of success.

Marriage outside the tribe is done when marriage partners are not available within the tribe but this is a last resort. Instead, a young woman might wait for an opportunity to become someone's second wife before accepting an out-group marriage offer. Marriage outside the race is the least preferred by the group. Having said this, it is also true that nowadays more and more Emirati men are marrying outside their race because they prefer the greater social freedoms such unions allow them (such as dining in the company of other non-related men and women) and because they can't afford the ever rising dowry prices. As many as 30% of Emirati men marry outsiders. However, divorce among these unions is estimated to be over 50%.

Children trust their parents to match them with a partner they will be pleased to spend their lives with. A search for a bride begins when the decision has been made that a son is ready for marriage. The marriage age has been rising from between the age of 13 and 15, to between 18 and 20. Some young men even finish a university education first and marry in their early twenties. Still, marriage is considered more important than education and if it has been decided the time has come, a person will be married.

Assessing a Prospective Bride

The women of the harem examine the family histories of their tribal relations. They identify some possible young women, weigh what they know about the women more carefully and debate their suitabil-ity. When they have selected one or two 'finalists,' a close, trusted and sharp female family member pays a visit to the girl's home. This female family member is not the groom's mother. Were the young woman or her parents to stop the proceedings, the grooms family would suffer a loss of face. Thus, it is preferable to have a less closely attached party negotiate the proceedings at this preliminary point.

The female family member might have to visit the potential bride's home several times before she is actually permitted to see the young woman. When she has and approves of the woman, the procedure advances to the next step. The women of both harems pay each other several visits. By this time everyone feels comfortable that an offer will be accepted since the ground would not continue to be prepared if there were indications otherwise. The almost ceremonial proceedings of visits between the harems provide ample opportunity for one party to withdraw without bringing shame or dishonour to either party or blackening anyone's face through a direct rejection. When the fathers meet, the groom's father extends a proposal of marriage to the bride's father. The bride's father cannot answer until he has consulted with his wife and relayed the offer to his daughter. The daughter may refuse the offer even this far along in the proceedings. However, if all agree to the union, the fathers pledge their word of honour to each other and the couple are irrevocably bound through that code of honour. It will not be broken.

The Contract

The couple must sign a contract *(mut'a)* and this signing may occur any time before the marriage is consummated. This is the chance for a woman to set boundaries as to what is and isn't allowable in a marriage. She can limit the number of additional wives and concubines her husband may take to zero. She can have a large divorce settlement fee written into the contract, thereby making it less likely for her husband to divorce her and she can specify that in case of divorce, she keeps any children realised in the marriage until a specified age beyond that given in the Koran. (The Koran states that in case of divorce, boys stay with their mothers until they are 7 and girls to the age of 9.) A mutawa asks the couple if they will take each other as husband and wife. They are in different rooms for this. The bride and groom sign the contract and are legally married though they will not join each other as man and wife until after the wedding ceremony.

The Dowry

The groom pays a dowry to his father-in-law. The amount of this dowry has been increasing over the years and can be as much as US$30,000 or more for the daughter of the royal family. In addition, the groom and his family bring numerous gifts of gold, jewellery, cloth, and rare or valuable treasures. These gifts are presented at engagement and wedding parties and are displayed before all the guests. Jewellery has traditionally been the most prized gift. In the past, the jewellery given was of silver, now it is of gold. A woman wears her jewellery comfortably and casually. It is a sign of her wealth and financial independence.

The Night of Henna

The month before the wedding is a time of preparation. The bride's body is repeatedly perfumed and dusted. New and more elaborate dresses are worn each day. The bride's hair is continually oiled, ambered and aloed; her clothes are scented with incense; and her eyes are heavily adorned with kohl and antimony. Henna is applied to her hands and feet to make them soft. Henna is a powder that is mixed with water to make a paste. The powder was once ground from dried leaves gathered from locally grown henna trees. Now it is purchased already ground and in packages from India. The paste is applied to the palms and fingers of the hands and to the soles of the feet. It is applied in elaborate patterns and allowed to dry. When it is dry and brushed away, the pattern has stained the soft skin. Henna is used in other parts

Emirati women display wealth through their jewellery. This woman can boast a substantial dowry.

of the Middle East and India. Patterns vary geographically. The Emiratis prefer intricate patterns of leaves connected by vines, or geometric patterns.

The Night of Henna precedes the final wedding day celebration. All the women of the harem gather for a great henna applying party. They must keep their limbs still and keep their hands and feet from bending or they will crack and ruin the design. Henna takes about an hour to dry the first time it is applied. It is applied repeatedly to make the design very dark and each time it takes longer to dry. The women are helpless while the henna is drying and so must be waited on virtually hand and foot while the process is happening. It is a festive night of pampering, laughing and joking, and great excitement over the coming event.

While the Night of Henna is a special festive occasion, wearing henna is by no means limited to weddings. Young girls henna their hands as frequently as girls paint their fingernails in the West. Many are quite accomplished at it.

The Wedding

Thursday night is the preferred wedding night because it is the eve of the Friday sermon in the mosque. It starts off the week long celebration during which the contract is signed. The Emirati wedding ceremony has become elaborate and expensive. The wedding is an opportunity to display wealth. It shows the groom's family's ability to look after the treasure of another family. The wedding takes place over the course of three days to a week. Wedding preparations begin once the bride has accepted an offer. This is the courtship phase during which the bride is kept more well covered and hidden than before.

The celebration was traditionally held in large tents, some set aside for the men, some for the women. Recently though, weddings were moved to hotel banquet rooms and professional musicians were hired to entertain the guests. The government has banned the use of hotels for weddings in an effort to limit the outrageous sums of money being spent on them. Weddings are once again being held in the large, traditional tents.

The celebration consists of music, dancing and dining. Music can be provided by modern professional musicians or by traditional folk musicians playing the drums and lute. Dancing will usually take the form of a traditional hair dance. Men form two facing lines or a large circle around a group of girls between the ages of 6 and 11. These girls cannot have reached puberty because while young girls can be seen by men, women cannot. The girls undulate their tiny hips and shoulders while swinging their long hair in circles so it whips about their heads. This traditional dance has been adopted by professional Arabic dance troops and can be seen on television. The wedding dowry is passed from the groom's family to the bride's. This consists of more presents of gold, jewels, and cloth. Animals are slaughtered and barbecued whole. Gigantic portions of food are served on large platters. Leftovers are sent to neighbours. The event is a grand show of hospitality for large numbers of guests being served by servants or other hired help.

On the final night of the celebration, the women escort the bridegroom to the bedroom of the bride. This room is located in the home of the girl's parents where the new couple will reside for about a week as a sign of respect to her family. Evidence of consummation will only be produced at the request of the groom's family. It is rare for such a request to be made.

The wedding is a great strain on the happy, excited bride. She is paraded about in elaborate clothes and draped in gold that grows heavy with the wearing. She must chat with numerous guests for an entire week with never a moment to herself. To be kept at such a high level of excitement and to be the centre of everyone's attention for such a long and continuous time is exhausting. But ask a young bride about it and she will patiently explain, "It is our way."

DIVORCE

A woman has the right to divorce her husband for impotence, desertion, inability to support her according to their agreement, or madness. A woman wants to have her right to divorce written in her contract, because it is not as easy for her to divorce as it is for a man. She must go through the courts and have a good reason for doing so beyond her personal dislike of her husband. Her purpose in life is to produce children, so one reason she would want to divorce is because she and her husband are not producing children together.

If she divorces her husband for impotence, he is allowed to prove her wrong by performing before three witnesses. If it is a true case of impotence, the man settles quietly. A divorced woman returns to her family. In the past she was considered a financial burden to her family, but now the government gives her a living stipend and she is not a burden.

A man does not need a reason to divorce his wife nor does he have to go through the courts. He simply says, "I divorce thee" three times and he and his wife are divorced. He may remarry his wife but limits are imposed on him after the third time when he must then wait 100 days before remarrying her. Divorce is not encouraged. Men and women seeking divorce are urged to reconcile.

TEMPORARY MARRIAGES

One of the seemingly hypocritical Muslim Arab practices is realised in the marriage contract – it allows for prostitution. A Muslim wanting to have illicit sex, enters a marriage contract with a woman, has sex, then divorces her and pays her the 'divorce settlement fee.'

He wants to keep such practices quiet because while such marriages are technically legal, the behaviour is not socially acceptable. The man still has his reputation and social standing to protect.

SEX

A few words need to be said on this topic. Limiting access to women causes them to be in constant focus. The lack of women in the Emirates also contributes to that focus. Exact numbers for the ratio of women to men are even less available than an accurate census by nationality. However with 60% of the population being comprised mostly of male labourers, even generous estimates cannot go over 30%. Sexual tension is high, like a constant underlying current. The group least affected by it are the Emiratis who consider this a normal and natural environment, with balanced numbers of men and women and common social mores to guide and govern their behaviour.

Chapter Five

OUT AND ABOUT

Eat of garlic until you are full
Eat of onions what you can find
Eat of radish tails as a habit
—UAE proverb

RESTAURANTS

The Emirates' three major cities have a selection of restaurants ranging from a corner juice shop serving fruit shakes to those serving fine Italian cuisine. Of course, choice of food and location of the restaurant are reflected in price. One of the best meals I've eaten was a breakfast of two large meat and egg sandwiches and three cups of coffee at a roadside hut for about US$.50. Fast food restaurants will cost from US$7.00–US$15.00 per person and an expensive meal with spirits could run from US$40.00 per person and up. This is not exorbitant given the high salaries earned by foreigners, but then it is not something to be done everyday.

Up until early 1995, you could not find a McDonald's restaurant because it is a Jewish corporation (Israel and Judaism are censored as completely as possible from the country because of the ongoing strife with Israel). Money did eventually open the doors to the chain and now everyone can order a burger and fries in any of the big cities. Elsewhere in the country one is unlikely to find much other than roadside huts serving Indian cuisine or no restaurants at all. One type of restaurant you will not see is one serving Gulf Arabic food. Limited resources and a hard life have hindered the development of a unique cuisine and many of the Emirati dishes are actually borrowed from other countries that have traded with them through the centuries.

Restaurants usually have family sections. These are upstairs or tucked out of sight. Single men, primarily labourers, are not allowed in these parts of the restaurant and the intent of the separation is to provide women with as much privacy and segregation as possible while in public. Women do not have to sit in these secluded areas, but in some restaurants, the male staff will be uncomfortable with a woman's decision to dine in the main area and will communicate that to her through looks and extremely fast service. The secluded sections may also make women feel more comfortable in public as they can't be stared at when they are tucked away.

MEAL TIMES

Breakfast is eaten between 6:30 and 7:30, before work or school. Work stops between 1:00 and 4:00 or 4:30. During this time the Emiratis, labourers, bankers, and shop keepers eat lunch and sleep. This custom is the most sensible for the labourers who are mercifully allowed to rest while the sun is at its hottest. Many foreigners working in the oil industry or education follow a Western schedule and only take an hour for lunch with work finishing for the day at 5:00. Those with a longer lunch break resume work in the afternoon and work until 8:30 or 9:00 in the evening, after which they have a small dinner. This is a schedule similar to that found in many Mediterranean countries and a healthy one given the local climate. In many ways the difference in schedules is useful for the Westerners since after work they can still run errands or shop. Further, the UAE is 4–12 hours ahead of the Western countries they do business with and a change in schedule would not facilitate communications with them.

Emiratis eat dinner later than Westerners are accustomed to doing, as late as 11:00 or 12:00 at night. However, restaurants typically follow a Western schedule of serving dinner from 6:00 to 10:00.

THE FUALAH

In addition to the three meals, breakfast, lunch, and dinner, described here, Emiratis also eat two other small meals called *fualah*. One of these meals is eaten between breakfast and lunch and the other is eaten between lunch and dinner. The fualah is a ritualistic meal performed for visitors because it enables the hostess to perform her duty of seeing the visit extends into a meal.

The fualah is also performed for festive events such as the birth of a child, religious feasts, the circumcision of a boy, and weddings. The food served consists of a variety of fruits, sweets, nuts and coffee. Perfumes and incense are also passed around as part of the ritual. Incense is placed in burners, lit and fanned until it is burning well enough to produce wafts of smoke. The burners are then placed under raised legs, dresses are drawn tightly around the legs, then the *abbaya* (black cloak) is securely draped over this so the women can absorb as much smoke as possible. If a woman is wearing a skirt and blouse, she will stand over the burner and pull her waistband away from her waist so the aroma can reach her blouse and hair. The women enjoy using perfumes, incense and dyes that are artistic or seductive. They are always applied to clean skin after a shower or ablutions for prayer.

RAMADAN SCHEDULE

During the Holy month of Ramadan, dining and sleeping schedules change drastically and Westerners are affected by the changes. Arabs eat before sunrise and after sundown but fast in between, taking neither food nor drink. Arabs' religious awareness is greatly heightened during this month and the Emiratis are far less tolerant of blatant deviation from their customs. It is illegal to be seen drinking or eating in public during daylight hours. Bars are closed or tucked away from offending sight. Restaurants outside of the hotels are closed until sunset and the blast of a cannon signals the breaking of the fast. This is called *iftar*. Most restaurants serve an elaborate buffet. Guests are poised over the buffet table and when the cannon sounds, signalling the fast may be broken, they dive in, piling as much food as they can onto their plates. This is not a time for reticence if one wishes to get something to eat, do not allow yourself to be pushed out of line in the frenzy.

Muslims commonly undergo weight changes during this month, either losing a lot of weight because they cannot accustom themselves to the change in eating schedule or, more likely, gaining weight because they eat so much through each night in an effort to make it through the next day without food. (Ramadan is discussed in more detail in Chapter Ten.)

SITTING

Upon entering an Emirati home you should remove your shoes. Shoes are seldom worn in the house because the floor is highly utilised as living space. Emiratis spend much of their time on the floor sitting, resting, cooking, eating, and caring for children. They believe sitting on the floor is good for resting a tired body. Resting is best accomplished on hard cushions because soft ones can cause the back to ache. The practice of sitting on the floor is *sunnah* or in accordance with the Prophet Mohammed's customs. It is thought to demonstrate modesty and be more directly in contact with nature. Some Emirati houses sport chairs, particularly the wealthy, the upper class and those who frequently receive foreigners.

There are three customary sitting positions. The first is the cross-legged position where the shins cross over each other and the knees rest on the floor. The second is with the legs bent and both knees pointed in one direction, one leg resting on top of the other. The third position is with one leg bent as in the previous two positions and the other leg drawn up, the knee pointing to the ceiling and the foot lying flat on the floor. Westerners are not typically comfortable in any of these positions for long and fidget back and forth alternating between them much to the amusement of the Emiratis. Feet should not touch the food tray. Emirati men and women cover their feet with the edges of their long clothing and you would probably feel more comfortable if you were able to do likewise. Protruding feet do stand out.

Two Emirati men sitting in the third position.

GULF CUISINE

Emiratis eat many foods that are similar to non-Gulf Arab selections such as lamb, chicken and mutton (adult sheep) cooked whole or prepared as kebabs (meat and vegetable skewers cooked over an open flame) and served on rice with a tomato and vegetable sauce. However, their other dishes are unique in that most of them are sweetened with the sugar from dates (their most abundant agricultural crop). *Bilaleet* is a dish of cold vermicelli noodles, sweetened and served with a hot, flat omelette on top. Pieces of the omelette are used to pick up the sticky vermicelli to eat. *Harees* is a paste of lamb and cracked wheat. Rice and meat dishes are flavoured with a mixture of cardamom, coriander, cumin, ginger, turmeric and saffron called *baharat*. Their breads, as with many dishes, are borrowed from cultures the Emiratis have had trade contact with. Thus, the flat bread called *mafrooda* is from Persia and *naan* is originally from India.

Using Your Hands

There is a proper etiquette to eating with the hands. Only the right hand is used because food is a gift from God and should be accorded respect. Dip your thumb and first and second fingers into the dish. Make a ball out of the food (this takes practice) and rest this on the two fingers. Push the ball of food off the fingers into the mouth with the thumb. Emirati women are able to do this without removing their *burkas* (veils) or using their left hand. They lift and pop food in with one swift, practised movement.

Where quality may not pertain in Emirati cuisine, quantity does. Two to three times as much food as can be eaten may be prepared as a sign of hospitality. The excess food is not wasted, but is shared with poor people or is eaten by the family and servants in the days to come. If you enquire of an Emirati about a dish or express an appreciation for one, you may be presented with a large quantity of it in a day or two. When you have finished the dish, prepare something from your country and return the full container to the Emirati. One expatriate I knew received a large platter of rice with a whole roasted camel hock in the centre. This is not an uncommon show of hospitality.

In an Emirati home, the family and guests sit on pillows. Guests visit for about two hours before a meal is served and linger about an hour after. It is a good idea to bring your host or hostess something small such as flowers or candy. Guests are served eldest to youngest with the younger people doing the serving. When guests are present, men and women eat separately. Children are only present if they know the guests well.

The men eat before the women but the women do not eat their leftovers. Instead, separate meals are prepared for both groups. A woman may eat with her father, brothers, sons, uncles and nephews when there are no guests. These men are members of her incest group, i.e., those men she cannot marry. If you are a woman and have been invited to dine with the men, be aware that you are considered the entertainment, not the guest.

Food is served in the sleeping or living areas and the majlis is used as a dining area only for guests. Food is served in platters on mats on the floor so one is considerably higher than one's food. Everyone eats using their right hand from the same large platters, but these are so big and the amount of food in them so great, neighbours are unlikely to bump into each other.

Some hosts and hostesses may provide guests with a plate and serving utensils with each dish. Go ahead and use them, Emiratis want more than anything for you to feel comfortable. The host or hostess usually serves the guest who should be prepared with two hands to accept the overflowing plate. It would be rude to refuse. The more food placed on the plate, the greater the honour being shown the guest. This can border on the ridiculous and you should not feel you have to eat more than makes you comfortable. The food is eaten quickly and in silence.

Eating Customs

Food is seen as one of God's greatest gifts and customs have arisen to reflect this belief. While eating, there is very little talking. However, there are ceremonial sayings at different stages of a meal. Everyone says *Bismillah* (in the name of God) just prior to eating. During the meal the host or hostess encourages everyone to eat more and says such things as *Billah alaich tihbshi* (by God you should eat) and *Ma habashtu* (you did not eat). You may need to indicate you are finished eating several times. When you are really finished say, *Akramch Allah* (May God honour you) or *Allah yin'am 'alaich* (may God bestow his grace on you). The host or hostess will end the meal with *Bil 'afiah* (to your health) to which you reply *Allah yilafich/yhannich* ('may God make you healthy and happy' to a man/woman).

Coffee

Coffee is served at the end of the meal. Coffee is the single most significant expression of hospitality in the Emirati culture. You should never refuse a cup as it implies an insult. The coffee will have been freshly ground, mixed with cardamom, and is unsweetened. Nowadays it is commonly poured from a thermos bottle but traditionally it was poured from a *dalla*, a brass pot with a long beak-like nozzle. Dallas can be found in the *souks* (markets). The Emiratis view them as junk but tourists think they are wonderful souvenirs. Shopkeepers price them according to what they think tourists will pay for them.

The coffee is poured into handleless demi tasse cups. Only about one third to half of the small cup is filled. Servers pride themselves on being able to hold enough cups for four to five people in the left hand while pouring and serving all of them without setting the coffee pot down. When you have had enough coffee, at least three helpings, shake the cup from side to side several times, otherwise the server will keep filling your glass.

You will almost always be offered coffee or tea when you walk into a business and always when in someone's home. There is no need to play coy with this group of people – accept it on the first offer. While relaxing over coffee after a meal you should say *Al hamdulillah* (praise be to God) to show your contentment. A water bowl and towel may be passed around for everyone to wash their hands.

When inviting Emiratis to your home, inform them whether men and women will be separate otherwise the man may show up without his wife. Even if men and women are separate, it is unlikely your Emirati guest will bring his wife. Serve a large variety of items to choose from, but do not serve alcohol. If you decide to serve pork, be sure and label the dish so the Emiratis know not to have any. Encourage them to have seconds and thirds. Do so more than once so that you make them feel welcome and when they leave for the evening, escort them all the way out of your apartment building or gate to their car. The front door is just not far enough.

NON-GULF ARAB CUISINE

There are numerous Lebanese restaurants in Abu Dhabi and Dubai and a few in Al-Ain. The food and service in these tend to be excellent and reasonably priced. Some dishes on the menu are *shish taouk* and *shish kebab* – skewered meat cooked over a grill; *hoummos* – a puree of chick peas, *tahina* – a sesame paste with lemon juice; *tabbouleh* – a mixture of tomatoes, cucumbers, cracked wheat, onions, olive oil and lemon juice served on shredded lettuce; and *dolmathes* – vine leaves that are stuffed with a rice mixture.

Diners sit at tables Western style and use silverware to eat with. It is still advisable to eat only with the right hand so as not to offend or disgust anyone. If you happen to be left handed then it is fine for you to eat with your left hand, just don't then get the right hand involved in the process. Some of these restaurants also offer the option of sitting on cushions at a low table – Moroccan style. If you select this option you may also need to request silverware. Waiters are politely out of earshot, but are there to refill your water glass or fulfil a request at a signal from you. Seating is gender mixed as is customary in Egypt, Lebanon, and other non-Gulf Arab countries.

Foul (pronounced 'fool') is an Egyptian dish you may see on menus. It is a paste made of fava beans that is eaten with pita bread. Emiratis view it as a peasant's dish and as such hold it in contempt. If an Emirati asks you whether or not you eat foul he or she is teasing you. Laugh good naturedly as it is meant in fun.

A STROLL IN THE PARK

Emiratis are proud of their parks which they refer to as gardens. They have them in every city, in particular in Al-Ain, which is also called the garden city. Some parks are for women only and most parks at least have women's hours when only women and children are allowed to use them. Emirati families can be seen in parks every evening and the foreign visitor is welcome as well. Some of these parks have restaurants with the usual fare described above under non-Gulf Arab cuisine. They will feature an Arabic singer(s) and men will get up from their tables and dance.

The women, seated apart from the men in the family section will not participate. It is truly pleasant to dine at these places surrounded by Arabic language and song, smells and ambiance. You may want to try the 'hubbly bubbly' a fruit favoured tobacco smoked from a large water pipe. Be careful though, it is strong and will make you light-headed if you are not accustomed to smoking it.

THE ROADSIDE CAFE

Along with Lebanese restaurants, Indian restaurants are the most numerous. Lebanese restaurants tend to be more upscale and more expensive than the average Indian restaurant, but hotels do design elaborate Indian dining facilities and a high price to go with them. Indian restaurants are more frequently the roadside cafes one sees everywhere. They serve mainly spicy Indian cuisine and cater to the labourers. Some foods you might find in an Indian restaurant are *biryani* which is chicken, mutton or fish cooked in mildly spiced rice; and chicken or mutton *tikka*.

Dining in these restaurants is a cultural experience in itself. The restaurant is a simple room usually having a dirt floor. Long metal tables fill the small room, with chairs or benches lined up around each table. The restaurant remains empty until the workers arrive en masse. Noisily they crowd in at the tables, food is served in platters almost immediately, the same for everyone. All talking stops as the eating commences. The food, shovelled into the mouth with the right hand, disappears in minutes and one by one the workers rise, wash their hands and return to their jobs. These restaurants serve a sole purpose, that of eating. They are functional rather than pleasurable, setup to refuel the body as a gas station would refuel a car.

A girlfriend and I once stopped at one of these, seemingly in the middle of nowhere. It was about midday. We were seated at the end of one of the long metal tables on an earthen floor. We asked for a menu and silverware. Both took considerable time to be produced as the waiter had to go in search of them. We ordered and our food was served almost immediately. We dawdled over our food and were still eating at one o'clock when two trucks full of men pulled up and unloaded their human cargo. Men crowded in and managed to find seats everywhere but at our table. As they silently ate their meal, they stared unflinchingly at us like children seeing something for the first time. The meal done, the workers left immediately. It was curious to me that in a life of so few pleasures. one wouldn't linger a bit more over one's meal.

WESTERN CUISINE

The hotels offer restaurants of every variety imaginable including Belgian, Swiss, Italian, French, and Mexican. You will be able to order cocktails, a bottle of wine to drink with your meal, and an after dinner cognac if you so desire. The privilege will be reflected in your bill. Entertainment such as belly dancing or live music may also be part of your dining experience. The quality and variety of food are usually excellent. This is a great way to spend a date and the person doing the asking will usually do the paying as well.

Hotels have been getting out of hand with their prices and service fees. You can expect a service fee on everything, even on top of another service fee. Unfortunately price is not necessarily reflected in quality of service. Frequently you pay five-star prices for three-star service. Be sure and complain. Recently in Al-Ain the bars raised their already exorbitant prices of beer. The Westerners boycotted the hotels and the prices came back down. The Emirates have a somewhat false economy and thus a private sector going ballistic with their prices and a transitory expatriate clientele not sticking around long enough to keep things in check. Prices are reaching a point where even the newcomer is alarmed and the best way to curb the trend is to refuse to pay their increasing prices.

Numerous fast food places exist everywhere in Dubai and Abu Dhabi. Al-Ain even sports a few. Food is usually ordered and picked up at the counter, though Pizza Hut provides table service. Often diners have the option of eating in the front room, where anyone may sit, or they may eat in the family room, usually located upstairs.

The American tradition of 'going dutch' where everyone pays for themselves is popular among many of the expatriates. The preference is to divide the check evenly by the number of diners but there are still those who squabble over the last dirham. Of course, there are other acceptable forms of etiquette regarding the check. One occurs in the pubs which follow the Irish and British custom of taking turns buying rounds. Reluctance to follow this tradition will not go unnoticed.

European style coffee shops are springing up here and there. Some of these even have outdoor seating that is comfortable to sit at in the winter months. These cafes serve Arabic coffee, espresso drinks, and regular black coffee; juices, sodas and mineral waters; vegetarian sandwiches; and a variety of pastries.

DRINKING

Drinking is a major pastime for many of the single Western expatriates and Christian Arabs. Families tend to be more involved in activities children can participate in, but this is not a hard and fast rule. One of the reasons Westerners drink so much here is that there is little else to do. Organised activities frequently centre around or provide a reason for drinking. There are numerous night clubs in Abu Dhabi and Dubai and most of the other emirates have a couple. Thus many of the obvious means for meeting other Westerners centre around the consumption of alcohol.

LEISURE ACTIVITIES

Sports are perhaps the number one alternative form of amusement. Most expatriates exercise at a gym or join a team sport out of sheer boredom, even if they hate to exercise. Available competitive sports are rugby, softball, soccer, and tennis. A few adventure businesses have recently opened and offer caving, scuba diving, rock climbing, camel riding, wind surfing, and dune buggying. These latter are expensive. There are also a number of yacht clubs and golf courses which frequently hold tournaments and award cash prizes. For the nature enthusiast there is a natural history club and if you get tired of listening to the lectures, your request to speak knowledgeably on a relevant topic will probably be met with enthusiasm. Many people purchase four-wheel-drive vehicles and spend a lot of time exploring the desert and wadis or experimenting with how much hard and adventurous driving their vehicles can withstand.

For expatriates who like their jobs (the higher the salary and the more time off given the easier it is to do this) and have the right attitude, living in the Emirates is a perpetual holiday. For others the perks must constantly be weighed against the frustrations of daily life (the stares, the boredom, the different attitude towards time, and multi-cultural contact). Some hate living in the Emirates because for them the perks don't counterbalance the frustrations. A few happy people belong to the first group and the rest fluctuate between the latter two, especially during the stages of culture shock. Those who land in the second group often stay and those who end up in the third finish out their contract and leave.

Another major concern for the expatriates is that keeping current in their professional field is difficult and requires great effort as opportunities are limited. Some people are able to study through correspondence and thankfully advanced telecommunications are making this easier for everyone.

Off the beaten track, there are many different classes offered and available time is just the thing for developing a new skill. Classes are

Exploring the desert in four-wheel-drive vehicles is a favourite pastime of the Emiratis, particularly after rain when new wadis can be found.

offered in ballet, karate, belly dancing, horse back riding, ice skating, and henna painting. Individuals offer private music lessons for piano, guitar, and wind instruments. You can check the classified sections of one of the two major newspapers to find an instructor.

Falconry

Falconry is a sport in which the Emiratis train wild falcons to attack small prey and bring the prey back to serve as the evening meal. In the past, this was not a sport, but the Emiratis primary means of obtaining fresh meat. Falcons can be bought at market or trapped (using live pigeons as bait) as they migrate south. Skilful falconers tame their falcons with a gentle touch, rewarding them with food to train their behaviour. One end of a line is tied to a falcons leg and the other end is held by the owner. The falcon is sent towards a bait made of the wings of a bustard from a distance of 100 metres or so. He is rewarded with a meal for attacking it. It is an art to train a falcon to be aggressive

87

enough to attack quarry and at the same time obedient enough to bring the quarry back to the master. The falcons are trained to catch bustards, hare, and other small desert animals.

When not hunting, falcons can be seen perched on their owners forearms. There are special forearm guards worn to protect the owners arms from the falcon's talons. When at rest, the falcon's heads are covered with a leather hood to shut out movement which might startle them. The hoods keep the birds as calm as if they had been sedated. Falconry is a winter sport beginning in October and ending in March. The falcons are released back into the wild at the end of the season.

Pearl Diving

Pearl diving was one of the Emirates' primary income generating industries before oil was discovered. Pearling vessels were made of wood and had one large sail. They anchored offshore and men dove for oysters. A diver wore his undergarment and pinned his nose closed. A weight assisted his descent and he quickly dove 20 or more feet to the sea floor where he gathered oysters with his bare hands placing them in a basket tied to a line held by another worker on the ship's deck. When he was ready to return to the surface he tugged on the line and was hauled immediately to the surface. Sharks, sting rays and inattentive shipside partners all posed death threats to the divers.

The Japanese development of cultured pearl farms devastated the Emiratis' industry. General world demand for pearls was satisfied by the perfectly round and even pearls produced by the Japanese. Still, natural pearls like those found in the Emirates are more valuable than cultured pearls and the Emiratis' industry continues today on a smaller scale catering to the smaller market willing to pay the higher price for the real thing.

MEDIA

The two major English newspapers are the *Kaleej Times* and the *Gulf News*. They are available in English or in Arabic and you can have them delivered to your house, pick them up on the street from a newspaper 'boy' before 1:00 p.m. or take your chances finding one at a book shop (bookshops usually run out early in the day). The *Gulf News* has a colour supplement that gives pictures and information on expatriate activities. It focuses on a different city or emirate each day of the week. Eventually your picture could make this supplement. Excellent coverage of events in the Emirates is found in *What's On*, a substantial magazine produced by Motivate Publishing and serving the UAE and Oman.

The Emirates have one television station which transmits two channels out of Abu Dhabi for eight hours each day. Most of their programmes are in Arabic with an occasional English or French programme. Scheduled shows are subject to change at any time and without notice. A cartoon may suddenly interrupt the rugby game you were involved in watching. None of the aired programmes will show politically sensitive material or anything sexually suggestive.

Many people, even the Emiratis, have satellite dishes on the roofs of their buildings. Channels they can beam in 24 hours a day are Arabsat, Star TV, VTV, CNN, and the BBC (Arabsat actually goes off the air at midnight or 1:00 a.m.) Of course, there is no way to censor these channels so censorship is up to the discretion of the viewer.

Video tape rental shops were doing a great business as long as the government could get by without enforcing international copyright laws. Fairly recent Western films were always available although copy quality couldn't be guaranteed. The pirate market came to an abrupt end in the summer of 1994 along with the 'for-real-this-time' outlawing of the pirated cassette market. New cassettes are now only offered at full price. Video tapes are harder to come by since newly opened video rental shops are having to stock their shelves from scratch. The good news is that while you'll pay more for your videos and cassettes, they are of much better quality.

There are movie theatres in some of the cities. Many of them cater solely to the Indian population. However, Dubai has seen a recent influx of new movie theatres showing only newly released Western films. These films are censored and shown at a very high volume perhaps to show off the cinema's stereo system or to drown out the 'illegal' sound of ringing mobile phones. These films are changed about every three weeks.

HOLIDAYS

Some holidays in the Emirates are set to the Gregorian (Western) calendar. These are New Years on January 1; the Accession of the President, Sheikh Zayed on August 6; and National Day on December 2. Other holidays are set to the Muslim Hijri calendar which is based on a 354 day year and begins in 622 AD when the Muslim Prophet Mohammed went from Mecca to Medina. The Hijri year is also divided into 12 months (12 cycles of the moon) and is 11 days shorter than the Gregorian year. This causes many holidays in the Emirates to occur earlier every year by 10–12 days. These holidays are only officially announced when a new moon is sighted. If you are planning to go somewhere during any of these holidays, you will want to book several flights on different days well in advance to be sure you are able to get a flight out. These holidays are very busy travel times.

A BIT OF 'CULTURE'

An occasional concert comes to town (Dubai or Abu Dhabi). Michael Jackson was scheduled for a show in 1994, but that one didn't materialise. Some do though and the expatriates flock to them for a change of pace. British Airways frequently sponsors theatre groups and, through the hotels, arranges dinner theatres. These are by and large British comedies relying on sexual innuendos for their humour.

Dubai and Abu Dhabi have a few art galleries which feature fine art of all mediums, from charcoal drawings and oil paintings to photography and sculpture done by locals and expatriates alike. Each emirate has at least one museum. These are usually located in newly constructed or renovated forts to give the visitor the feel of life in the past. On display are weapons tribes once used against each other, Koranic verses and carrying cases, equipment for the pearling and fishing industries, carpets, musical instruments, chests and clothing.

The fort in Ajman has a wind-tower, the traditional means of cooling a house. The tower is open at the top on all four sides to catch any available breeze. Two short walls cross each other at the top of the building and breezes are funnelled down the channels these make into the room below. Shelves or cabinets are built halfway up the wall to store perishables. The system works incredibly well even on the hottest summer days when it seems there is no breeze at all. These towers have been replaced by air conditioning in almost all houses and business. Unfortunately, living in air conditioning causes many people to walk around with summer colds since it is so efficient in spreading germs.

Chapter Six

SOCIAL VALUES

TRADITION AND HERITAGE

The Emiratis were, and many still are, a nomadic people. They lived in small family groups travelling from oasis to oasis (an underground spring providing a small amount of surface water and vegetation for shade). Their separateness from other people and the isolation of the desert instilled a patience and physical endurance that enabled them to survive in their harsh climate. There are unwritten laws amongst these desert people that strengthened the group. These rules also made survival possible and are strictly adhered to even today. The values described below are those of the Bedouin and while modernisation has affected the Emiratis to a great extent, it is a surface level change only. Social beliefs and values are the slowest aspect of any culture to change. So, when in doubt, follow traditions to be safe.

BEDOUIN VALUES

Bedouin values and their code of ethics are ideals Emiratis still prize and try to emulate. They admire today's Bedouins who continue to live as desert nomads. City dwellers aspire to emulate the mentality that passively endured the harsh desert climate; that politely offered hospitality to strangers passing through; and that enforced cruel punishment to any who deviated from the strict rules of the group.

Hospitality

Hospitality may be the single most important law of the desert. Without it, people travelling in the desert away from their groups would die. Even poor people are required to feed and shelter strangers and guests for an obligatory three days. The guest may leave after a few days without ever having stated his name or business, as it is rude for the host to ask. Without this hospitality, an individual would not survive the desert, nor encounters with other people once he left the family or tribe. Even a fugitive, a person shunned from their own tribe, or a person guilty of a crime against their host is taken in and treated as a guest of honour for the obligatory three days.

The guest is taken into a majlis, a meeting room with carpets and pillows on the floor (see Chapter Two). Food is served in platters on the floor and eaten using only the right hand (don't expect utensils). The left hand is strictly for hygiene functions.

Coffee, the main symbol of Arab hospitality, is ground in a brass mortar with a brass stick. The sound of brass striking brass signals to people nearby that a guest has arrived. Everyone stops what they are doing and gathers in the majlis to greet the guest.

Arab hospitality is prevalent even in a modern society and an Emirati will never leave you in need. An invitation for coffee will extend into dinner and perhaps an overnight stay as well. I have come to rely on this hospitality when I drive long distances. My second hand car breaks down from time to time in the desert heat. The first Emirati to come by always stops to help me. Once I thought I had enough petrol to make it the 130 kilometres home – I didn't. Within five minutes a car stopped and a *mutawa* (religious leader) siphoned gas from his tank to mine as his two bodyguards looked on.

Modernisation has affected the value of hospitality. An urban home with a gate and a closed door have replaced the open and inviting tents the Emiratis once lived in. Segregation has become stricter because opportunities for contact with strange people who have conflicting values abound. This can make visiting awkward. Great shows of hospitality are now saved for special occasions such as weddings, funerals, and the month of Ramadan. A host's honour, reputation and face all depend on the lavishness of the presentation which represents how hospitable they are.

Outdoing each other in displaying hospitality has, in some places, gotten out of hand. Weddings are the most frequent and obvious display. The hosts invite everyone they know (uninvited guests are also welcome), feed the guests and send them home with huge amounts of food too, purchase the latest gown from London, and proudly display the bride in all her splendour before the guests.

Generosity

One of the five pillars of Islam, giving alms to the poor, instructs Muslims to be generous. The wealthy give money and food to their poorer neighbours. Sheikh Zayed donates as much as 30% a year of Abu Dhabi's income to poorer Muslim countries. Abu Dhabi, the wealthiest of the Emirates, also shares its wealth with the six other Emirates in the form of funds for education, hospitals, road construction, and other subsidies. You are very likely to hear stories proudly told of a past relation who was generous to the point of personal ruin. These stories tell of a man who, upon seeing yet another stranger approaching, quickly slaughtered his last goat and rushed out to offer the newcomer what meagre amenities he had left.

On an individual basis, Emiratis frequently extend invitations to outings in parks and wadis and give gifts at every opportunity. It is rude to refuse their gifts and offers because a refusal does not allow them to carry out their good intention. In some situations, the Emirati will call a thing a 'gift' while the Westerner applies the term 'bribe.' It is a fine line and small wonder many Western countries have attempted to eliminate gift giving in professional situations.

Hidden Emotions

The Emiratis say, "It is shameful for tears to fall, but tears in the eye are like pearls." They experience the same range of emotions as other people, but it is shameful for them to show tears. They are experts at showing a 'poker-face,' giving a blank stare as they weigh and balance their thoughts before speaking. They do not trust people who do not look them directly in the eye and their own gaze becomes more steady the greater the depth of their emotion.

An Emirati will seemingly become more agreeable the less he or she agrees with you. A close look will reveal an almost imperceptible underlying stillness set in the jaw and a blank stare in the eyes. Quickly review which of your words or actions caused offence and apologise. This will be greatly appreciated. You will almost always find an Emirati willing to negotiate conflicting views or desires but a wall will come up if you must have your way and will be fortified by your insistence.

I claim cultural ignorance when I see I have caused offence and am always forgiven. Once, when explaining the word 'successor' to a group of students, I began, "Well, when your present ruler dies ..." There was a collective intake of breath, still faces and faces quickly converting tears to stillness. I apologised profusely, told them I could see I'd done something wrong and found another way to define the word. Emiratis believe that referring to someone's future death wishes it upon them. Had I not already had my students trust and respect, I might not have been shown the brief glimpse of the depth of offence my words had caused. The incident, however, was forgotten as quickly and completely as it was forgiven.

Relationships

Personal relationships are extremely important to the Emiratis. In the past, an occasional visitor brought news from other family groups. Such news consisted of greetings, marriages, births, deaths, illnesses, tribal feuds, and anything delineating status relations among the people. Today this kind of personal news continues to dominate the newspapers, taking precedence over war, drought, and famine in the world. "Sheikh Zayed receives fax from Sultan Qaboos of Oman wishing him a speedy recovery from his recent cold," scream the headlines. Western newspapers save such little tidbits for their society pages, but the Emiratis make no pretence as to the significance of this kind of information in their lives.

Emiratis feel friendship deeply. Once a friendship has begun, the Emirati will invite his or her friend over for meals frequently, take them on outings in parks and oases, and treat their new friend like family. The friend is expected to drop whatever he or she is doing at the least invitation. The inability to accept an invitation due to work or other time constraints will prompt further invitations until one is finally accepted.

In general, expats simply do not spend the amount of time in each other's company that Arabs do. It is advisable to proceed with caution in forming friendships. Be certain of your motivation and desire in forming the friendship and your availability to sustain it. Too many hard feelings have preceded the newcomer in this regard.

Even shopkeepers will grow attached to you at a rate and to a degree which may be uncommon in your own country. For example, when you return to purchase a carpet from a shop where you have purchased before, the shopkeeper will greet you with open arms, as though you were a long, lost friend. You will be seated and served coffee and you will discuss pleasantries for fifteen minutes or so before you state the purpose of your visit. This runs contrary to the hurried pace of business as conducted in many other countries, where the purpose of a visit or phone call is usually stated up front.

Tribal Relationships

> I and my brothers against my cousin;
> I and my cousins against the stranger.

The Bedouin have a patriarchal society. Their loyalties are to their kin and are felt strongest for the closest family members. Loyalties are less strong the less closely related people are. In the past, extended families travelled together. All members of the group were able to trace their lineage to one common man. As these families grew in number, they joined other related family groups and formed a tribe. In force, they were able to protect themselves from the threat posed by other tribes.

Group cohesion was the key to the survival of these tribes, so absolute conformity to the values of the groups was demanded. Behaviour that lent itself to group cohesion was acceptable and good, while behaviour which did not was dishonourable. Group members who broke the groups code of ethics or in some way refused to conform, brought shame to the group and the group turned them out. Without group protection, an individual could not survive in the desert.

The value of group conformity is adhered to even today. As a teacher I have found sometimes that large classes of Emirati students are difficult to control. I've found that gently singling out those with the most obvious behaviour problems brings shame upon them and makes them conform to proper classroom behaviour.

Peace within a tribal group was imperative. Aggression was not allowed because it could result in harm being done to a group member, which would diminish the strength of the group. Emiratis are a very peaceful people. They consolidated seven tribes into one confederation 25 years ago, settled their internal boundaries, and have lived peacefully together ever since. An Emirati's loyalties are to his family first, then to his tribe, and then to the confederation.

A Bedouin man with a Khonjar knife strapped to his waist.

Value of Men to the Group

Men had to protect the group from other warring tribes. The more protection a group had, the stronger they were. Because men added immediate strength to the group, while women only had the potential to produce sons, men were more highly valued than women. When a boy was born, there was dancing, feasting and celebrating. However when a female child was born, little was done to mark the event.

To say the Emiratis were a warring people paints a bloody picture that is not entirely accurate. Death was avoided since the death of group members weakened the group. Tribal feuds took the form of raiding each others' herds. These raids provided more food and more cattle for the successful raiders and as a result, added strength to their group. A stronger tribe would not raid a weaker one since to do so would cause them shame. The goal was not to eliminate each other, but to gain strength and hence, power over other groups.

The need for protection (in this case of the flocks), caused bravery to be a highly valued characteristic in the male Bedouin. The lack of bravery brought shame to the Bedouin and also to his family and his tribe. Suppressing physical or facial expression in the face of physical or emotional pain was a sign of self-control and courage and was highly valued. One ritual that tested a man's bravery was the public group circumcision of boys just reaching puberty, 8–10 years old. Boys were circumcised at this age because they were able to withstand infection better than a newborn. They were expected not to cry out in pain while having their foreskin removed, but rather they were to shout with joy. Nowadays this custom is more frequently performed in hospitals one week after birth.

A man who lived up to the ideals of the group was considered honourable. Such a man was renowned for his hospitality and generosity. His blood was purely Arabic and he could proudly trace his ancestry all the way back to the Prophet Mohammed. He sired many sons and worked without undue labour, for example, tending flocks. He was a dignified man but quick to exact revenge when his honour

99

was slighted. He bravely defended the group when called on to do so and the women of his family were chaste, their hand in marriage a sought after prize. Such a man was greatly admired and still embodies the ideal aspired to today.

Honour

A man's honour is called *wijh*. When a man loses his honour his face is blackened. Honour belongs to a man through membership in a tribe. It requires him to defend what is his (his land, flock, women, and other possessions) and to respond to the demands placed on him by his family or the tribe. His honour could be lost by his inability to keep and control his possessions including his women. Thus, the women under his protection could affect his honour through their actions. A lack of modesty in dress or behaviour such that the woman would arouse other men would bring shame to the man. This power women wield over a man's honour causes him to both respect and fear his women.

Value of Women to the Group

The value of women, as in so many cultures, lies in the woman's ability to produce sons. The children a woman bears belong to her husband. Since children, sons specifically, will add to the strength of the group, it is desirable for a woman to produce children for the group. Emiratis value in-group marriage because it increases the number of people in a group.

Female circumcision is still widely practised in this region. Many Emirati women question this practice but the men still support it. Evidence for this comes from men who state they would not marry a woman who had not been circumcised. This puts Emirati women in a bind. They are only able to marry Emirati men for two reasons. First, Emirati men are the only ones who have equal or greater status to them and are worthy of marrying. Second, Emirati men are the only men they have any access to and to catch one, a young woman must follow the socially acceptable mores of the culture. Change comes slowest for the women.

Time

Many Western and modern Asian cultures could be called slaves to time. They buy, save, keep, take, spend, and use time in a host of ways. The Emiratis on the other hand are not as concerned with time. In the desert there is no sense of urgency or haste and no sense of future. The attitude is that tomorrow will come, yesterday was, so why be concerned with any time other than now? As a result, Emiratis are not prone to planning out the future or the course of their lives in the way many other cultures do.

It can be quite disconcerting for the expatriate to say, "See you tomorrow" and hear *Insha'alla* (God willing) in response. This refusal to forward plan results in big projects being approved at the last possible moment and being carried out practically overnight. Quality and precision have been known to suffer as a result.

The difference in conceptualising time is a cause of frustration for many expatriates. Deadlines are made and set as absolutes in the mind of the expatriate, but they are rarely met. This causes the expat to hurry up and wait a lot. If these delays frustrate you, do not show your frustration, since becoming emotional or losing patience will result in a lengthier wait. If you anticipate delays from the start, you will save yourself much grief.

Contact with the West has forced the Emiratis to adjust to Western time concepts to some extent. Work schedules are set and timetables are made. However, even if a store or office is scheduled to open at 4:00 p.m. it may not actually open until closer to 4:30. Such things as the cycle of the moon can now be accurately determined with scientific instruments, yet Ramadan begins when a mutawa in Saudi Arabia sights the new moon himself, not when the West predicts it will appear. Emiratis have made other concessions to time in keeping with Western conceptualisation. Planes usually take off and land when they are scheduled to and movies begin on time. These are superficial conveniences, in reality, time just does not matter so much. If something is not accomplished on Monday, it will be accomplished on Tuesday or Wednesday – Insha'alla. Your disappointment will be met with the expression, *mafi mooshcola* (never mind, it doesn't matter). So, relax, when you think about it, it really doesn't matter.

Courtesy

As in many cultures, one should never point the bottoms of one's feet at another person. Give and accept things with your right hand. When entering a room say, *salama lai kum* (peace be upon you) to which all present will respond, *wai lai kum salam* (and upon you be peace). This will interrupt a business transaction, a conversation, or a grammar lesson. Human relations are held to be of utmost importance, so the foreigner must learn to accept and participate in these interruptions.

Following the opening greeting, all men shake hands with the newcomer and touch the tips of their noses about three times before parting. The number of nose touches reflects the depth of feeling the parties have for each other. Women kiss each other on the cheek – once on the right cheek and three times to dozens of times on the left, again reflecting the parties' depth of pleasure at seeing each other. Men and women do not touch each other and are rarely in each others' company. Next comes a series of questions about the health of each other and each others' family. For example:

A: How are you? Fine?

B: *Al-Hamdulilah* (Thanks to God).

A: How is your family?

B: *Al-Hamdulilah.*

A: How are you?

B: *Al-Hamdulilah.*

A: How is your brother?

B: *Al-Hamdulilah*. How are you?

A: *Al-Hamdulilah* ...

Even when the Emiratis speak in English to a Westerner, they carry out this discourse. So while the language is English, the culture is Arabic. The first speaker answered his own question because, since greetings and responses are always positive, the speaker knew the answer. I often find myself racing along trying to accomplish an inordinate number of tasks only to come up against this discourse. It is as if someone were asking me constantly to stop and count my blessings.

Wasta

As personal relationships are so important to the Emiratis, it would follow that who you know is far more important than what you know. *Wasta* is the clout you have by virtue of who you are or who you know. Wasta opens doors, generates necessary official stamps and signatures and generally moves things along a little more quickly. Expatriates do not as a rule have wasta, but they may know someone with wasta, which is almost as good. Westerners may earn wasta in some circles. For example, frequenting the same stores and businesses regularly, especially if they are small, will bring automatic discounts and better initial prices. The store keepers will be genuinely happy to see you whether or not you buy anything and you may come to feel the same way about them.

Some large companies employ a man who has no specific job title but whose job it is to provide wasta to newcomers. This man knows the ins and outs of society and can make your settling in a lot easier. Be aware that he is taking a cut in many of your purchases. However, working independently will not save you any money since you will not be able to negotiate as good a price on an item as he can. In other words, he is earning his share while making life easier for you.

POINT OF DISCUSSION OR TABOO?

Practically all Emiratis are Muslim and so are as much as 95% of the rest of the population. Muslims pray five times a day and tend to be conscious of the teachings of the Holy Koran between times. Putting harmful things into the body is against these teachings. Drugs and alcohol are topics to avoid or to treat with care when questioned by an Emirati. Religion, politics, and sex are also sensitive topics because the foreigner's view is usually different and more liberal than an Emirati's. If you do not feel you can politely listen to their views without comment, you might be better off indicating you are uncomfortable discussing the topics. This should prevent further attempts to engage you in a taboo discussion because the last thing an Emirati wants to do is make you feel uncomfortable.

There are numerous acceptable topics of discussion. First and foremost is the topic of family. Enquiring about family will please an Emirati, though if you are speaking to a man, refrain from enquiring about the women in his family. This is bad manners because it implies that his women are loose.

Food is a safe topic. An Emirati will be happy to describe the kind of food he or she eats and how it is prepared. Don't be surprised if you are then brought a favourite dish. The Emiratis burn incense and blend perfumes endlessly. The musky smells are a delightful part of daily life. An Emirati will like being questioned about their special or favourite blend of perfume. Finally, medicine is a topic that will keep a conversation going. Emiratis have concocted family medicines that have passed from generation to generation. They are able to tell you about many different natural medicines and they have numerous true stories about curing people. If you exhaust these topics, do not worry, Emiratis are also comfortable with silence.

PROBLEMS OF MODERNISATION

Many, though not all, Emiratis are wealthy. Money has made life easy in some respects, but it has brought with it its incumbent problems. Oil money has provided the Emiratis with comfortable, air conditioned housing, cars, and office jobs. The Emiratis are now growing up without learning to endure desert conditions. When the oil runs out, hence the money, they will be unable to return to the traditional life the desert can support. The government has embarked upon a massive effort to educate its people and promote tourism for this eventuality. A further complication is a fast approaching end to their fresh water supply. Even if the Emiratis wished to return to a traditional life, they could not because of the shortage of fresh water.

In the past, families were always together in the desert. They often had little to do, so much time was spent enjoying each other's company. Now fathers are often away on business and servants do any work that needs to be done at home. The women, having little to do, shop a lot. The men, having little responsibility, and plenty of money, drive brand new Nissan Patrols and Range Rovers around the desert or sit and talk in a shady area. Some also indulge in Western influences such as drugs and alcohol. Family values are still very much intact for most of the Emirati population, but for how long remains to be seen.

Most of the country's hard labour is done by Pakistanis, Afghanis, Indians and Baluchistanis. What this results in is men doing work for which they may not even have concepts. For example, the man doing the electrical wiring for a newly constructed building is likely to have lived most of his life without electricity and the man driving the taxi may have never even been a passenger in a car until he came to this country. A brand new apartment building I moved into had not been cabled for telephones, though it had been cabled for satellite reception. Up came the newly laid sidewalk and after about a month we had telephones. The Emiratis do not seem bothered by the poor workmanship, perhaps because in many cases they can simply purchase a new house in seven to ten years when their current one falls apart!

Westerners have brought their expertise and their non Muslim values. Since the Emiratis still need the foreigners' expertise, they are tolerant and accommodating of their behaviours and values. The five-star hotels are the expatriates' playgrounds. Muslim Arabs are not allowed in parts of these hotels. The problem for the Emiratis is that many of their men do frequent these places, but wasta protects them from repercussions. The Emiratis are trying to change the make-up of the population as a solution. They are attempting to hire more Muslim Arabs (Lebanese, Egyptians, Palestinians) whose values are similar to theirs. An added bonus is that the Emiratis can pay this group of Arabs less money than they can a professional worker who comes from a wealthier country and demands more.

OPINIONS

Thinking for oneself and having an opinion is valued among people who value individualism. Group oriented people think not in terms of themselves but in terms of the good of the group. This group relies on the Koran to inform their opinions and guide their behaviour. Critical thinking and problem solving abilities are not necessary when all the answers can be found in a book. You may be disappointed by some of the answers you are given to intentionally thought provoking questions since average young Emiratis all seem to have the same answers. It can sound like you are being given a lot of party propaganda. Critical thinking and problem solving skills are being introduced into curriculums, but the content is extremely censored and the process is slow. While Star TV, CNN, and the BBC are available in their uncensored form to the Emiratis and may spark curiosity in some, they encourage fundamentalism in others.

FATALISM

The Emiratis do not believe they are in control of nature or the things that affect them or their future. Problems or lack of advancement at work are due to bad luck rather than anything the Emirati might or might not have done. This is not to say the Emiratis do not work for what they want, they do. However, if they don't achieve their goals, they don't blame themselves, rather they attribute their failure to having been God's will and trust that God wished them to have or do something else. This religiously based philosophy is much different to that of many of the guest cultures. Many expats are practically addicted to accomplishment and self-advancement and see the Emiratis and others who believe in fatalism as lazy, while the Emiratis see their efforts to control and direct the future as futile or worse, sinful.

These different orientations were recently highlighted for me. In a job interview I had to explain why I'd left a previous position after only six months. My reasoning was that the job had proven to be a step down and that there were no opportunities for me to advance. The interviewer looked puzzled, so I tried explaining in different ways. He finally stopped me and said, "I understand what you are saying, I just don't understand your way of thinking." He offered me the job anyway but the point is, that allowing for each others' differences must go both ways.

DEATH

When a person dies, the body is adorned as it would be in life and placed on its right side facing Mecca in a trench dug in a hole. The trench is blocked with pebbles and the hole is filled with sand. The survivors do not wear cosmetics, oils, incense, perfume, or jewellery. Friends and relatives bring food for the immediate family for three days and are in turn offered coffee (but not food) as a sign of renewed friendship. Men seldom visit gravesites and women never do.

There is no mourning period for a widower, but a widow is secluded for four months and ten days. If she looks at a man who is not part of her incest group during this time, she must immediately bathe in order to purify herself. Other relatives mourn for a much shorter amount of time and grief is hidden in public. A student came to me after having missed a week of classes and said, "Miss, I am sorry for missing class, but my mother died last week." I was nearly reduced to tears at the thought of it and I told her I was sorry for her loss. She matter-of-factly thanked me without the least outward sign of sorrow.

Chapter Seven

SETTLING DOWN IN THE UAE

FIRST COME

Arrival and entry into the Emirates is relatively straightforward. Your visa will be waiting for you at the airport, where you have agreed to meet your sponsor. An official behind a desk holds the visas and calls out people's names to step forward to get them. When you have yours, proceed to passport control where you get in line according to your country of citizenship. Baggage is then picked up and you proceed to customs. Customs will search your bags for weapons, drugs, and pornographic or politically sensitive material. Video tapes are temporarily held for censorship (permanently if they are too offensive). Video tapes are rarely overlooked by officials so don't expect to sneak your 'questionable' videos in. When your tapes are returned to you, they may have sections of film or sound edited out of them or black strips covering alcoholic beverages, body parts, and other items offensive to Islam.

Your sponsor should be waiting for you just beyond customs. There are now six international airports (Abu Dhabi, Dubai, Sharjah, Ras al Khaimah, Fujairah and Al-Ain) so be clear in communicating your arrival destination. Your sponsor will either be an employer, a friend residing in the country, or a five-star hotel. Anyone not entitled to reside in the United Kingdom or not holding a Gulf Cooperation Council (GCC) passport must have a sponsor to enter the country. Most temporary visitors are entitled to a one month visa. People with the right to reside in the United Kingdom may enter the UAE without a visa for one month and extend their stay up to two more months. Those with GCC passports may enter and exit the country without a visa.

Employment visas are obtained through a local sponsor and are good for five years. However, your employment visa will be cancelled when you terminate your employment with your sponsoring company. Visa sponsorship procedures are subject to change, either becoming more relaxed, in an increased effort to encourage tourism, or more strict with the desire to exert greater control over the population.

Employees may find it difficult to change companies once they are working in the country because the law requires they leave the country for six months before being permitted to change companies and re-enter. People who opt to remain illegally may have their picture published in the newspaper as a warning to other employers not to hire them. If you hold a residency visa, you may enter and exit the country without obtaining permits or stamps. However, some employers, particularly those with government affiliation, require you to obtain their permission to exit and re-enter the country. Failure to do so can be justifiable cause for dismissal and deportation.

If your passport bears an Israeli stamp, you will not be permitted to enter the UAE. You can exchange a passport bearing an Israeli stamp for a 'clean' one before applying for a visa. This problem may crop up in other Islamic countries as well. To avoid it altogether, you can request officials in Israel give you your stamp on a separate piece of paper and not put it in your passport at all. Israel is censored out of many aspects of life in the UAE. Movies featuring Jewish actors, producers and directors such as Yul Brynner and Barbara Streisand are not usually available. World maps on the walls of travel agencies sport black ink where Israel should be and Jewish people are not allowed in the country. It is not possible to book a flight to Israel by any route from the Emirates. (See Chapter Ten for more on strife with Israel.)

FIRST SERVED

At some point as you are trying to enter the country, an Emirati may very likely step ahead of you, even if you are a woman. Lines are definitely a Western concept, though they do exist in the Emirates. Emiratis are not governed by the equality of first come, first served that many people know, but by gender and nationality. Female nationals come first, then all other women (though Western women will probably be taken ahead of Eastern women), then national men, and finally all other men. However, the unwritten rule of women before men seems to be changing in relation to the national men who, with more and more frequency, put themselves ahead of all but national women. It is best to bite your tongue and allow the national to go ahead of you, especially as you are trying to enter the country, a privilege that could be denied if you enrage someone important enough. It is likely that the Emirati is someone important because being that the population is quite small, many hold high government positions.

PHOTOGRAPHS

One of the difficulties of being a photographer in the Emirates is your limited subject matter. One must be sensitive when taking pictures of people. Always ask permission. Men should not take photographs of women, especially not the Emirati women. Emirati women should not be approached by a man at all since this can be considered harassment. A woman's best defence when harassed (and she decides what harassment is) is to act hysterical. All men in the vicinity are suspected of harming her. The government has recently intervened on behalf of women because of harassment complaints. Men who harass are called 'Eve Teasers.' They are arrested and their picture published in the paper to humiliate them and discourage the behaviour.

While photographs of people can often be difficult to obtain, photographs of the scenery and animals are not. Many amateur photographers have found endless fascinating subjects to photograph in the Emirates and have honed their photographic skills there.

(The photographs contained in this book were obtained with the subjects' permission.)

FREE ITEMS

While many items and services in the UAE are exorbitant, many other things are surprisingly free. As of this writing, there is no airport tax; you will not pay for the cart you use to get your bags out of baggage claim; and customs will not charge you for any of the electronics you bring in. You don't even have to pay for the censorship of your video tapes. Your hotel should have a van waiting to pick you up (they will make up for anything free in the price of your room and meals) or else your sponsor will be waiting for you.

Most importantly though, Dubai's port is duty free. At other points of entry, import tax officially runs between 4% and 20%. However, as with many economic regulations imposed at an international level (such as the copyright laws), in practice they are not uniformly applied. Over half of the goods which travel in and out of the UAE do so duty free. Thus, goods pour in and out of the country at a terrific rate. Electronics, 22k gold and hand made carpets can be picked up in Dubai's markets for very reasonable prices. More on this topic can be found in the sections on shopping and doing business.

GETTING AROUND

Directions

The use of street names and numbers has not caught on well and where it has, it has not done so with a great deal of consistency or standardisation. Thus, you will soon become familiar with directions such as these:

"Turn right at the coffee pot R/A; go thru the 2nd R/A; after 2.2 km you will come to a short bush in front of a camel crossing sign, turn R ..."

Directions like these work because there is so little to see in the blinding white desert expanse that the smallest sign of civilisation or life takes on relevance. Abu Dhabi is laid out in a grid with street names marked. There is often more than one name per street, the one on the sign and the one many people use to refer to it. Maps may reflect either name so you will need to learn them both. Dubai is under great construction at the moment (and has been for years) and directions for getting around are more likely to go like this:

"Do you know where the old trade centre road used to be? No? Okay, how about the road that used to ...?"

It is not a good idea to ask directions from people on the street. A request for help cannot be refused even if the person is unable to help you. You will probably be sent off in the wrong direction and sent in a different direction by each person from whom you ask directions.

Taxis

Taxis are numerous and inexpensive. Taxis are required to have meters, so you do not have to negotiate a price. Dubai taxi drivers have stubbornly and successfully resisted this mandate and are also charging outrageous fees. Know your destination and how much it should cost to get there. Have your money ready to give to the driver when he stops. If he argues, advise him to get a meter.

Most taxi drivers in the Emirates are from the Indian subcontinent. Their knowledge of foreigners is limited to movies and stories they've heard. Often their assumptions do not have much basis in fact or reality. Whether positive or negative, reality does not seem to affect their assumptions. These assumptions are that all foreigners, and particularly Westerners, are rich and that the women are loose. In order to gain some of those riches for himself, a driver may take a roundabout route to your destination. He may also 'forget' to turn on his meter and charge you a higher price than you would have paid on arrival. Of course, if he honestly forgot, he may very well charge you a slightly lower price as well. Tipping is not customary, however, people from countries where tipping is the norm do not seem to be able to easily give up this practice and some taxi drivers may be slow to give change, in the hope you'll let them keep it as others before you may have done.

Everyone who takes a taxi, male or female, young or old, has a bad experience at some point. There are some precautions you can take in order to avoid having too many of them: sit in the back seat; do not make eye contact with the driver; remind him to turn on his meter if he has forgotten; limit your conversation; be polite but firm in communicating your destination and no more; and speak with authority as though you know where you are going and the best route for the driver to take even if you do not. If the driver does not appear to know where he is going, get out and take another taxi. It is less safe for women to take taxis at night especially outside of city limits – if at all possible, don't do it.

If a taxi driver tries to engage you in conversation, ignore him. Many taxi drivers will test boundaries as to what you will and won't permit. When crossing cultures there is so much that can be misconstrued and misunderstood that people need to determine the sphere in which they are comfortable operating and make that clear in their interactions with strangers. This becomes particularly important in the Emirates because of all the different cultures encountered each

113

day. Until you have been in the Emirates a while and can decide how much contact is comfortable for you, it is better to err on the side of caution when dealing with other nationalities.

Driving

Many expats opt to drive. Sponsors may offer their employees interest free loans for the purchase of vehicles or may even provide their foreign employees with vehicles, if the job requires the employee to travel from one site to another during a work day. A car will suffice for getting around since the surface roads are in excellent condition. Many people prefer four-wheel-drive vehicles for camping and recreation. It is necessary to wash your car regularly and it is a good idea to rust-proof the vehicle. Car washing stations are numerous as are the labourers who will wash your car every day for a mere dh100 a month (about US$30). Fuel for the car is cheap because it is subsidised by the government. You will not have any difficulties finding gas stations in cities or on the Dubai to Al-Ain road. However, you will have a harder time finding stations elsewhere and those you do find are sure to be closed at night. It is a good idea to keep a filled can with you.

Licenses

International driving licenses are not recognised. Obtaining a license is fairly simple for US and British license holders who simply complete forms and provide the department of vehicle licensing with pictures. A license is then issued to the requester. People of other nationalities are much less fortunate (unless they have an important Emirati sponsor to assist them) because they have to take a driving test. To take the test, you get on a bus with other people also taking the test. The bus follows a car which candidates drive one after the other, accompanied by policemen who pass or fail them. Passing is arbitrary, usually about three people in a bus load actually pass. Some people may take the test dozens of times before they are passed. An

One of the more unusual sights you may see on the road in the Emirates.

important and respected Emirati sponsor who is interested in having you pass can help you take the test ahead of the rest of the bus load and ensure that the formality of taking the test will result in a pass. As part of the ritual, before you can take a driving test, you must take a driving course.

You must always carry your license and registration with you when you drive. Police stop traffic from time to time to check for licenses and registration. Sometimes they are looking for someone who is wanted for a serious crime. If you cannot produce your license and registration, your car will be impounded for 24 hours. You may have it back by producing your documents and paying the fines and impounding fees. You must also have third party insurance. This is calculated according to the year and model of your car. Third party insurance is all you will be able to get on an old car. In desert conditions, old is six years or more. You may want to consider this when purchasing a used car. Most vehicles in the Emirates are white. White reflects the sun so people think their cars will be cooler. When it is 125°F, shade is the only thing that is going to make a difference in how hot or cool your car is.

In general, driving is atrocious. This is partly because driving laws and speed limits are not enforced and partly because there are many drivers new to the concept of driving. Accidents are frequent, particularly in the congested downtown areas and fault is often split between drivers if the policemen can't decide who should be charged or if an Emirati is at fault. Because of the frequency of accidents, one may wish to drive a large, new vehicle such as a four-wheel-drive. In addition to being safer, it is useful in the terrain outside of the larger cities and for women in discouraging young Emirati men from running them off the road. Women drivers are fairly common, though they are not often seen driving large model four-wheel-drive vehicles. Some Emirati women have licenses but many also have drivers. So, while some of them can drive, they are not often seen at the wheel themselves.

Traffic Accidents

If you are ever in an accident you may move your car to the side of the road, but stay at the scene. Leaving the scene of an accident is illegal. The police will decide who is at fault and what property damage needs to be reimbursed. When you have paid your fines and fees, you will be given a letter from the police giving you permission to have your car repaired. Repair shops will not touch your vehicle without this permission. It is illegal for them to do so and could result in the closure of their business and deportation for both them and you. If anyone is hurt or killed in a car accident, someone will be arrested. This person is most likely the ablest bodied person whether or not he or she is at fault. Fines and prison sentences will be sorted out in time, but you do not want to be in jail through this. You will need somehow to get yourself to the hospital if required, seek legal advice, and find an Emirati with wasta. If you are in an accident involving an Emirati, you will most likely be found to be at fault (for being in his country). In

When driving in the Emirates beware of camels on the road – an unexpected encounter can be costly and dangerous.

an accident involving a death, dh70,000 blood money is paid to the deceased's family regardless of fault. Insurance companies may refuse to pay if you are at fault, even if you have such coverage.

Outside of the big cities you will encounter livestock on the roads (or off roads). If you hit an animal, you are responsible for reimbursing the owner for the value of the animal. Camels can easily cost US$10,000. However, an accident with a camel is often fatal for both the camel and the occupants of the car because on impact, the camel's legs are hit out from under it and it's body lands on the cab of the car crushing the cab and the cars occupants with its weight. Stories are numerous of Bedouins letting their older camels roam near the freeways so they will be hit and the Bedouin reimbursed. More and more fences are in place to keep livestock off the roads and it is hoped the laws will change so the owner is fined for allowing the animal to stray onto the freeway, but to date this is not the case. Your best bet is to drive carefully.

117

A colleague of mine hit and injured an older camel. The owner of the camel took this man to court and was awarded a settlement of dh10,000 (about US$3,000). Pleased, the camel owner was leaving court when my colleague said, "I'll take the camel." The judge thought this entirely fair and made the owner hand the camel over to my colleague who sold the animal at market where he was able to recoup dh7,000.

Drinking and Driving

A lot of alcohol is consumed in the Emirates. Westerners may obtain licenses to purchase alcohol (or through word of mouth may locate the well known but illegal warehouses in Fujairah and Ajman that don't require a license). The license allows them to purchase alcohol and transport it to their homes only. Possession of alcohol when not in transit from the liquor store will result in a person's arrest if caught. An Italian acquaintance of mine borrowed a car and had an accident while driving it. An unopened bottle of whiskey (not his) was found in the back of the car and the Italian went to jail.

If you are in an accident and you have been drinking, you are in a lot of trouble. If no one has been injured, some consider it wise to walk away and then claim ignorance of the law when you do come back in a dead-sober state to take responsibility. You may at least avoid the lashings and prison stay. Many people drive home after a night out but smelling alcohol on your breath is all that is required for a policeman to put you in jail. It is simply not a good policy to drink and drive in the Emirates.

PUBLIC TRANSPORT

The major cities have a few buses. These tend to be operated for specific groups of people living in compounds on the outskirts of the cities; for students on their way to and from school; or for limited areas of town. Smaller vans operate a bus service between Al-Ain and Abu Dhabi; Abu Dhabi and Dubai; and Dubai and the northern emirates.

The bus service is only a few dollars. These buses are usually full of sweaty, male labourers and this may be uncomfortable for women travelling alone. There is not a bus service between Al-Ain and Dubai. You should be able to negotiate a taxi fare for this route of between dh175–250 (US$45–70). Better yet, you may rent a car for dh100 (about US$27) a day and cover your trip there and back. The telephone books are half in English and half in Arabic. Consult the yellow pages when you are interested in such things as car rentals but do not wish to pay hotel prices. Hotels can meet your every need, but they also charge much higher prices for their efforts than businesses not located in hotels.

WALKING AND CYCLING

Walking is almost impossible. When you are outside, you do not even have to move to be drenched in sweat during the summer months. Besides the unbearable heat, city blocks are long and cities are very spread out. Men may be able to do a little more walking than women, who will often be harassed by passing drivers. Cycling is not a transportation option for most people. A very few labourers ride them and an even fewer number of expats who are cycling enthusiasts ride them. Cycling is dangerous because car drivers don't have much respect for those on foot or on a bicycle. Also, the sun and heat are merciless and you must be careful not to exert yourself too much in this kind of weather.

EXERCISE

Expatriates often exercise indoors at one of the five-star hotels. These often have up to date weightlifting equipment, stair climbing, and running and rowing machines. They usually have pools that can be used for swimming laps. Hotels charge an annual fee for membership. This fee varies for each city and hotel. Many hotels have a personal trainer on staff, an aerobics instructor, a tennis coach, a golf pro, and possibly a martial arts instructor. An additional fee is charged for any classes offered by the staff. Most people join a club. They are useful for meeting other, non-work related expats, for alleviating the boredom, and for alleviating the stress of culture shock.

POLICE

The police should not be an intrusive presence in your life unless you give them cause to be. You will frequently see several police vehicles parked at roundabouts. Police will be standing watching traffic or talking to each other. All members of the police force are Emirati, as are the customs officials and government workers such as post office employees, and visa and immigration clerks. All employees at Etisalat, the telephone company, are also Emirati. You will on occasion see female Emirati employees, they often work in enclosed offices to assist women with their business. A female police officer wears a uniform similar in colour and trim to her male colleagues; different from his in that the bottom half of her uniform is a floor length skirt and her head is covered.

The secret police, all male, are everywhere. Certain conspicuous clues should tell you when you are in the presence of an agent: his plush, air-conditioned Mercedes taxi is one example. If you are stopped by the police, be extremely polite, apologise for your traffic error and explain that you don't usually do such things and won't do it again in the future. You just may be forgiven.

POST OFFICE

Postage is expensive, but the service is reliable. Letters usually take less than one week to arrive at their destinations. The post office is one of the few places open straight through the day. Official hours are from 8:00 a.m. to 6:00 p.m. Saturday through Thursday and lines are often long. Men will want to go from 2:00 to 5:00 p.m. when lines are short or nonexistent, or else they could have a female friend mail their letters. If there are no postal workers present, wait, they have probably gone to pray and will return in 10–15 minutes.

Mail is delivered to post office boxes usually located at one's place of employment. Packages will not be delivered. You will receive notice of receipt of a package. You pick it up at the post office and take it through customs. They will search your package for questionable material as described previously.

THE BUREAUCRACY

The administrative system in the UAE was borrowed from other Arab countries and is rather complex. Many people are employed in jobs that are superfluous by some standards. All the extra help results in a lot of red tape. This means some documents you must obtain will need to be stamped and signed by many people who will barely even glance at what they are signing half the time. The other half of the time they will examine your papers carefully and make you wait in order to show you how important they are. When this happens you might cope with it by observing how creatively it is done.

The process of applying for telephone services, obtaining driving licenses, making large purchases, and requesting complex services consume large blocks of time as a result. You should get your business done in the first half of the day, while employees are at their most productive. If at all possible, have someone who has been through it accompany you through the process. A woman assistant is preferable to a man since she won't be made to wait in lines where she is liable to tempt the thoughts of men.

PAYMENT

How you pay for items and services depends on where you are. Markets and small businesses usually only take cash. You may write cheques off your local bank account for utilities such as the telephone, at hotels, and at some businesses that sell large items such as appliances, furniture, curtains and carpets. Your use of a cheque may get a reaction (a frown or a smile since they are so infrequently used). Credit cards are always welcome at hotels and stores selling gold or carpets. More and more stores are prepared to accept credit cards, but don't expect to use them off the beaten track.

SHOPPING

Food can be purchased in grocery stores such as Spinney's or Choithram's or in the souks. The grocery stores have good variety and prices. They may even have more of a variety than you are used to at home because goods are shipped in from all parts of the world. The open-air markets sell local fruits, vegetables, fish and meat, incense, and herbs used for medicinal purposes.

Purchase fish early in the day because it does spoil in the heat. There are many different kinds of fish to choose from, most will probably be unfamiliar to you. Stationary stores sell plastic fish charts to help you identify what you see and experimenting with all the different kinds can be fun. Once you've purchased your whole fish, you take it to a nearby 'gutter' to have it cleaned. Meat is cut directly from the fresh carcass as you order it. Most Westerners prefer to purchase meat in the grocery stores.

A roadside pottery souk – an opportunity to bargain for household items.

Dry goods such as household wares are purchased in indoor souks or small stores located on all the major and minor streets everywhere. You can also find old rugs, weapons and jewellery, scarves, incense burners, and imported treasures from India in these shops. Other individually owned and operated shops sell books, shoes, clothes, etc. Modern shopping malls abound in Dubai and are beginning to spring up in Abu Dhabi as well. Finally, both Dubai and Abu Dhabi boast duty free shops at their international airports that are making record breaking profits. When a lipstick costs US$30, it is no wonder. 'Duty Free' does not equate with low prices, it means, rather, high quality goods can be sold for prices that do not include duty costs or taxes. This is a bit of an oxymoron in a country where most goods can be purchased tax and duty free.

Bargaining

Customers are always expected to bargain. Shopkeepers and vendors will usually drop the price. If they won't, move on, you will find the same item elsewhere. There is no hard and fast rule for how much of a percentage to come down when bargaining, but retail prices can be dropped significantly. Bargaining is one of the cultural differences that seems to consistently bring those who aren't used to it into a culture shock dip. They begin to wish they could just go to a store where prices are actually marked on the goods and there is not a hassle. These stores also exist and some people won't shop anywhere else.

The only workers who are tipped are the man at the grocery store who carries your bags to the car and the porter at the airport. Tip dh1 per bag. When making large purchases in small towns and villages, you will often be pushed to take the item immediately and pay later. The shopkeeper is sure to make the sale this way and there really isn't far for you to run in this country, so the store owner knows you will be back to pay. You will also find this trust applied at stores where you frequently shop if you have forgotten to bring your wallet.

At a Choithram's, where I shopped about once a month, I was always given a great deal of assistance. One man unloaded my cart, a second man rang up the goods, and a third packed my bag. The one packing my bag frequently left an item out which I didn't discover missing until I arrived home. The man ringing up my goods sometimes rang in the wrong price and the man unloading my cart occasionally left my bags from other stores in the cart. All honest mistakes. Between watching all three of them, I never was able to catch all the mistakes and would have to go back to the store for my missing milk, bags, or money due. The store was always happy to rectify their error but I was not always happy to run back. Once, when a package of bacon (an expensive item) had been left out I simply decided not to go back there any more. Unfortunately, it was the only place in town to purchase bacon so I returned a month later and continued to shop there. Much, much later a store manager came up to me and asked me if I ever got the bacon I'd left behind. I said no but was sure they had forgotten about it. They gave me a package of bacon. That day was a real bonus because the guy packing my bags also gave me their cleaning supplies that had been on the counter.

Western Clothes

There are countless tailors whose labour is incredibly inexpensive. Men and women can have suits made to fit for US$40 or less (not including the cost of material). Choose your material carefully, it should be heavy or light enough for what you are having made. Your tailor will make the garment you request whether you've chosen the right material or not and you will have to pay for it. While the choice of material is up to you, a good fit is up to the tailor. You should not pay for a garment until you are happy with the way it fits. Once you've paid, the tailor will not touch the item again. This applies for other services as well as tailoring, so be sure you're satisfied before you pay.

Ready made garments are available, though they are considerably more expensive than tailor made clothes. These come from England,

India or the Philippines. Clothes from England tend to be either conservative or trendy. Conservative clothes are often too warm for the climate and trendy clothes, in addition to having a short life cycle, are often poorly constructed. Clothes from the Philippines are likely to be brightly patterned and covered with buttons and spangles. Clothes from India are the traditional Saris. These are made of silk or cotton, fibres which are excellent in the desert heat. They can be dressy or casual. While dressing in the sari is perhaps the most comfortable of all the choices, this outfit is seldom worn by expatriate women.

If you are dressing for a night on the town, bare shoulders and form fitting gowns are common for women and men will wear nice suits or even tuxedos. Your trendiest clothing will be perfect for wearing to the discos and you will want to bring plenty of clothes for the beach and for exercising. Dress is more conservative where there are likely to be Emiratis or other Middle Eastern and Eastern men such as the movie theatre, shopping malls, souks, and in the villages and towns of the smaller emirates. If you are in doubt as to what to wear, cover your arms and legs in loose fitting clothing.

Emirati Clothes

The Koran encourages modesty in dress but does not require the extremely discreet garb worn by the Gulf Arabs. Dress is more a matter of custom. The Emiratis' religious belief is that the form of the body should not be apparent for men or women. They also believe in dressing very well in public. At home, more casual Western dress may be worn, even jeans. For a while many Emiratis were discarding their traditional dress for Western style clothing, but the pendulum has swung back in the direction of conservatism and it is most unusual to see them in Western clothing.

Emirati clothes for men and women are tailor made. The women's clothes are heavily embroidered. Women wear a traditional, long straight gown called a *kandura* that has a round neck with a short slit

125

down the front. The slit and the sleeves at the wrist are embroidered. The material is plain or patterned. These gowns are worn by older women and by the younger generation as well. However, the younger generation has been influenced by Western styles. Blouses and long skirts commonly replace the simpler one-piece gown. These can be folded and tucked in numerous ways; have long, flared hems and sleeves; be covered with buttons, ropes, and strings; and be completed with platform shoes in the latest London style. Of course, heads are covered with scarves (black ones if the woman is Emirati) and black *abbayas* over the dress. Under the clothing the women wear baggy cotton pants held up by a drawstring at the waist. The pants, called *sirwall*, are heavily embroidered at the ankles for decoration.

Older women and married women wear a mask that covers their eyebrows, nose and mouth. The masks are adornments that do not actually conceal much. They are worn to beautify and are cut to enhance a woman's positive features while hiding her blemishes. They emphasize a woman's eyes and have probably contributed greatly to the exotic quality of eyes in Arabia. The covered parts of the face become another erogenous zone, covered except for intimate encounters. Cuts to the mask are made to the length and width of the eye slits, the corners of the eye slits and the length of the sides of the mask. Especially daring women cut their masks so that their upper lip is barely covered. These masks are black and may have embroidered decorations on them. Women wear them comfortably and they become less intrusive as you grow accustomed to them.

This traditional garb came about as a matter of prestige to distinguish 'free' women from slaves. Older women who have worn them their whole lives have surprisingly few wrinkles. The current generation of young women seem to be discarding the mask, but there are still plenty of very traditional women who don the mask at puberty and remove it only for their husbands. A child whose mother wears the mask may never see his mother's face, but he knows her eyes and smell well enough to single her out. The eyes tell a great deal. In my classes, about 20% of the women were completely covered except for their eyes. I could pick those students out by name from a crowd of women as easily as I could those students only wearing a scarf.

Men wear a white shirt-dress called a *dishdasha*. It comes to their ankles and can be very elegantly yet subtly embroidered. They cover their heads with a white scarf called a *ghotrah* that is held in place with a black rope called an *agal*. Sandals adorn their feet. For ceremonial occasions, men wear a dress-like overgarment called a *thob*. This garment is usually black, often with embroidery along the edges. When Emirati men leave the country on vacation or for business, they may wear Western clothes.

EDUCATION

Expatriates with school age children have numerous choices among the many private schools. Each school caters to a specific clientele and offers a curriculum similar to one found in the home country. Some schools require students pass a screening process before they are admitted. Restrictions such as country of origin can also affect admission.

Schools offer numerous after school activities from Scouts to sports to tournaments and competitions held in neighbouring countries. However, their exclusivity can limit them in providing cross cultural opportunities. Often students of other nationalities attending a British or American school are fairly Westernised.

Students may experience adjustment problems typical when changing schools and countries. And just when you thought you were safe, children are exposed to the same socialising problems they would encounter in the home country: drug and alcohol problems and teen pregnancies. Encountering these problems may occur at an earlier age than back home because there is so little for children to do in the Emirates and parents are sometimes busier socialising themselves than they were back home, leaving children more in the care of house help than might be customary for them.

127

Dubai and Abu Dhabi look easy on the surface because everything is available. It is easy to be lulled into thinking you are not in transition. Schools and organisations offer orientation programs to assist newcomers. Parents who involve themselves more in their childrens' lives, interests and projects may be more successful at keeping their children out of trouble just as they would be at home. Select a school that meets the needs of your children. Services for children with physical or mental disabilities are almost nonexistent, particularly in higher grades. Tuition can be as much as US$10,000. Companies usually pay this fee. In fact, some companies buy blocks of space in a school for the children of anticipated newly arriving employees. Find out in advance, it certainly isn't a fee you want to be paying out of pocket.

HOUSING

Your sponsor should provide housing for you. Consider this issue up front when you are negotiating your contract. Housing is limited and the cost of renting (only citizens may purchase) is high. Additionally, housing is paid in six month or year lump sums. There are a few apartment complexes (in Dubai in particular) that rent on a month to month basis.

Sharjah, only a 20-minute drive from Dubai, is an option for expatriates who work in Dubai. Apartments in Sharjah are considerably less expensive than in Dubai and more readily available. There are a couple of reasons for this. First, there is only one main road open between Sharjah and Dubai at the moment and traffic is congested. Second, Sharjah has been a dry emirate (meaning the commercial sale of alcohol is completely prohibited) so the night life is tame compared to Dubai. Living in Sharjah simply pales in comparison to living in Dubai.

Expatriates live in villas or apartments. Buildings are constructed of concrete. Workmanship tends to be poor and electrical fires sometimes occur within the walls causing smoke damage. Doors and windows are not well set and keeping sand out of the house is a daily battle. Every room in the house has a door, including the kitchen. Floor plans are improving with new construction but many places are laid out with a hall as the central area with rooms set off from it here and there. This is not conducive to entertaining, a thing many expats do a great deal of here. Expatriates are known to have long vacations and their houses may be watched and robbed while they are gone. As this happens all too frequently, insurance agents have begun to allow coverage where tenants may only be gone for a one month period in a year.

ELECTRICITY

Only 220 volt electricity is available. You can purchase electrical converters for your small 110 volt appliances. Appliances used this way have a short life span and you will eventually end up purchasing new appliances using 220 volts. Bathrooms do not have outlets in them.

FURNITURE

In the not so distant past, furniture choice was very limited. Emirati taste tends to favour glitz and a few years back one was hard pressed to find a bedroom set that did not have flashing neon lights and a stereo system in the headboard. Nowadays there is considerably more choice. You can find anything from second hand to IKEA. You can furnish your house in old Portuguese carved wood furnishings or wicker. You can search the 'nickel ads' or save up for the finest money can buy.

A few entrepreneurs have caught on to the idea that Westerners like antiques. They are manufacturing them at a great rate and charging increasingly higher prices for them. Look around, however, and you might actually be able to find some treasures that others have considered to be junk and thrown out. These treasures are complemented well with a few Persian carpets purchased at the Sharjah souk.

PUBLIC RESTROOMS

In the past, the women used to go out into the desert in one group and the men in another twice a day, once at dawn and once at dusk when the light was fading and they could not be seen. Now public restrooms are as available everywhere as they are in any developed country. The toilets are of two types. First there is the Eastern porcelain bowl inlaid in the ground. There are spaces for your feet on either side of the bowl. Toilet paper is almost never available because it is assumed people use their left hand to clean themselves. Westerners usually carry around a supply of tissue. The other type is the pedestal style toilet 'seat.' As with many borrowed Western conveniences, the 'seat' was adopted not for its usefulness, but because it is Western. Footprints on the toilet seats are an example of how things borrowed from the West are adapted.

BEACHES

With few exceptions, the UAE's population is concentrated on the coast. The Emiratis walk and drive on the beach but do not swim in the ocean. Outside of the cities people can walk on the beaches wherever they please. Dress should be conservative, particularly if you are alone or with only one or two other people. In a group, while you may be watched, you will be left alone. Women alone in the Emirates anywhere will attract unwanted attention. Married women are fortunate to always have a man with them and life is easier for them in this respect. Single women would do well to travel with a male friend.

Within the city limits there are public beaches. While it is legal for you to go to these beaches, it can be uncomfortable. They tend to be frequented by single subcontinent men though these men are occasionally accompanied by their families. The women wisely stay covered. The men strip down to their underwear to swim. Westerners are so outnumbered at these public beaches it is too uncomfortable to go because they are stared at by everyone. Expatriate women have a particularly bad time of it because even in male company they receive undue attention.

As a foreigner your options for going swimming at the beach are therefore limited to finding a beach with a group of friends well outside the city limits or going to a big hotel and paying to use their beach. This can be expensive, as much as US$14 per person for day use. The hotel provides towels, beach umbrellas, showers, and sometimes a hot tub. The beaches are clean and enclosed by wire mesh.

MONETARY UNIT

The monetary unit is the dirham which is set to the US dollar. One US dollar is equivalent to 3.65 (buy) – 3.68 (sell) dirhams. Banks are usually run by Indians with an Emirati serving as chairman or featuring in a figurehead position. The reason for this is that the Koran advises against usury. An obsolete meaning of usury is the practice of lending money for interest and the practice thereof was designated a low status occupation. The current meaning of usury is lending money at an extremely high or unlawful rate of interest. So while the Arabs accept the practice of lending money at interest, they place low value and respect on it as a profession.

A bank or small exchange businesses can convert your money in the form of a cheque which can be sent by registered mail to your bank in your home country or which can be wired to another account through the bank. Wirings, however, are costly (about dh60/US$16) and all too often faulty. The difference in time is about 10 days through the mail and 2–3 days for wiring, if all goes well. Keep all receipts until money has been posted to your account in case you have to trace your deposit. When in a foreign country it is advisable to keep the bulk of your income in a stable currency. There was a closure of a large bank in the Emirates in 1990–1991. Funds were not insured and people lost a great deal of money.

TIME
Local time is GMT + 4. England is four hours earlier than the Emirates and the US is 9–13 hours earlier. There is no daylight savings time change.

USEFUL NUMBERS
Area Codes:
Abu Dhabi city – 02
Al-Ain – 03
Ajman, Sharjah and Umm al Qaiwain – 06
Dubai city – 04
Ruwais and Jebel Dhanna – 052
Fujairah – 070
Ras al Khaimah – 077
Country code – 971

Emergency
Abu Dhabi and Fujairah:
  police – 999
  ambulance – 998

fire – 997
Everywhere else:
all – 999

For operator assistance dial 100 and for directory enquiries dial 180 or 181

HEALTH

Many Emiratis use herbs, seeds, roots, spices, plants, and prayer to heal. For example, a sauce made of thyme, fenugreek, frankincense and kheel is used to clear constipation. Frankincense is also eaten to cure a stomach ache or burned so the smoke can cure a headache. When all attempts to heal an ailing person fail, a firehealer may be called in to brand an afflicted person. The fire healer applies the tip of a hot rod to an ulcerated or infected area. These practices are still common among villagers and old people and some remedies may always be trusted over other methods throughout the society.

The UAE government has had modern hospitals built, equipped them with the latest medical instruments, and staffed them entirely with Western doctors. These new hospitals are exclusively for the Emiratis and health care for them is entirely free. Staff in hospitals are accustomed to the Emirati women not wanting to undress for male physicians or male patients for female physicians. Western female doctors are in great demand. When an Emirati has to be admitted to the hospital for care, he or she is accompanied by the entire family who camp out in the patient's room and in the halls.

Foreigners receive care at hospitals that are a bit older and whose equipment and services are a generation removed from the latest and greatest found in the Emirati hospitals. Many, but not all, of the staff were educated in the West. They may or may not speak English. Get concrete recommendations from other expats on which doctor to see for your particular ailment. You may be saved the frustration of searching for a medical professional with whom you feel more comfortable. If you want care from the Westernised Emirati facilities, you will have to obtain written permission from a highly placed sheikh.

Some optional vaccinations you may want to get are typhoid, tetanus, and poliomyelitis. Cholera is not a problem in the Emirates and the cholera vaccine is purported not to be terribly effective anyway. You do not have to worry about plague, but there are many feral cats, some of which carry rabies. They search for their food in the garbage bins. Try to avoid them. Some accounts advise you to take precautions against malaria. In three years, I only knew one person to come down with malaria and he got it on a vacation in Madagascar. The Emirates is too hot and dry most of the year to be a breeding ground for mosquitos. Check with your embassy or airline for a government advisory regarding the current situation.

Hepatitis A is a possibility, but the vaccine lasts such a short time (2-6 months depending on the strength of the dose) it is often not worth bothering about. Hepatitis A, diarrhoea, and food poisoning may result from poor food hygiene or poor sanitation. Avoid eating food from fly infested restaurants. Drink bottled water – it is worth the cost to be safe. People who live in developing countries for a long time develop immunities and can relax some of their eating and drinking practices. Short time travellers do not have time to do this.

Brucellosis is an illness carried by cattle and transmitted to humans through milk. Proper milk pasteurisation will kill the germ, but out in the desert milk is brought straight from the animal to the dinner table. When you are offered tea or coffee in the desert, accept the coffee. Tea is usually served with milk while the traditional Arabic coffee is not. When the germ is transmitted, it results in undulant or maltese fever characterised by a general malaise and hot and cold shivers similar to malaria. It is not usually fatal, nor is it curable and like malaria, it will recur throughout one's life.

Tap water is often safe to drink, but from time to time it is not. You can never know what will accidentally get in it. Water is usually stored in tanks on roofs. If the tanks are not clean, worms, bacteria, and other visible intruders will come out of your water faucet. One year many people in Abu Dhabi began complaining of an inordinate amount of hair loss. The government stopped using a new water purification chemical they'd been experimenting with and the hair loss complaints stopped.

— *Chapter Eight* —

LANGUAGE

ARABIC OR ENGLISH?

Arabic is the official language of the Emirates and is used on all official documents. However, English is the most common spoken language. The conglomeration of so many people from differing nationality and language backgrounds creates a need for a common language. The language chosen is the one the greatest number of people speak and that language is English. Most highly placed officials or highly educated Emiratis are fluent in English and in Arabic and switch back and forth between the two languages with ease and finesse.

Many shopkeepers speak both Arabic and English in order to cater to the greatest possible number of customers. Most non-national Arabs speak both Arabic and English and a large percentage of Eastern and subcontinent expatriates speak at least two languages – their native tongue and English or Arabic. The monolingual groups tend to be the Western expatriates who only speak English and the nationals who only speak Arabic.

LEARNING ARABIC

For the native English speaker, learning Arabic is rather difficult. Arabic pronunciation is wildly different from English. Arabic contains many sounds not made in English, that even with practice are difficult for the English speaker to produce. The most difficult of these sounds are those made at the back of the mouth and throat (the glottals). Arabic is a stress-timed language making its rhythm predictable and regular, while English reduces and blends sounds together to fit its stress pattern. Intonation patterns of the two languages are used to convey meaning in similar ways, for example, both languages have rising intonation in questions.

Arabic grammar is markedly different from English. Verbs come before subjects and have particles added to them to change the sentence in various ways. Adding *laa* or *maa* to a verb makes it negative. Pronouns can be prefixed or suffixed to the verb and still other particle additions are used to refer to the future. The verb is always gender specific, indicating whether the person speaking, the person being spoken to, and the person being spoken about are male or female. These particles are not only added to the beginnings and ends of words but can be placed in the middle as well (called infixing).

Learning to read and write in Arabic is another hurdle, since the script is so different from English. Arabic letters are beautifully formed curves and lines bearing no resemblance to English. They are written from right to left in cursive with the letters within words connected to each other.

The Arabic alphabet has 28 letters, 22 consonants and 6 vowels. It has eight vowels and diphthongs as compared to 22 vowels and diphthongs in English. There are three short vowels that are not written because they occur in predictable patterns so Arabs are able to read words even with these vowels missing. However, encoding words into script without these vowels causes confusion among readers and writers when script is being translated from English into Arabic. Your own name will be spelled and interpreted in translation any number of ways.

Numbers

English borrowed the Arabic numeral system of using one symbol each for 0 through 9 and adding new place values for tens, hundreds, thousands, and so forth. These numerals are written from left to right and have different symbols from English:

1 *(wahid)*   6 *(sitta)*
2 *(itnain)*   7 *(sab'a)*
3 *(talata)*   8 *(tamaniya)*
4 *(arba'a)*   9 *(tis'a)*
5 *(khamsa)*   10 *(ashra)*

CLASSICAL ARABIC AND DIALECT

The Koran is written in classical Arabic and so the Arabic language is considered sacred. It is used for all writing, for formal discussions and speeches, and for news broadcasts. Its grammar is more complex than that of any of the dialects and 50% of the vocabulary found in the Koran is not in everyday use. Few foreign words are incorporated into Arabic because Arabic has such a large vocabulary it makes coining new words easy.

People with a good command of classical Arabic are highly respected. This is equivalent to saying Arabs have a high respect for literacy, literacy being synonymous with classical Arabic. One would think this respect for literacy would foster a high literacy rate but it does not, because classical Arabic is so very difficult to learn. A solution would be to replace classical Arabic with a dialect, but there is great opposition to changing anything that comes from the Koran. A standard language helps to unite Arabs from so many nations and changing the standard would cause a linguistic splintering that would add to existing political and cultural differences.

Dialects are used in ordinary, everyday conversation and in films and plays. There are five dialects falling into groups by geography. Gulf Arabic is spoken by people from Saudi Arabia, Yemen, Kuwait, Bahrain, Qatar, Oman, and the Emirates. This dialect is intelligible to Arabs in Egypt, Sudan, Lebanon, Syria, Jordan and Palestine. However, the Iraqi and North African dialects are different enough to cause difficulty in comprehension. The main differences in dialects are in vocabulary. Arabs resort to classical Arabic when they don't understand each other but foreigners do not have this luxury and feel they are dealing with yet another language.

THE BEST LANGUAGE?

Arabs have an intense love for their language. They view their language as one of their greatest cultural achievements. However, this pride is felt only for classical Arabic and does not extend to the dialects. Arabs go to school to study classical Arabic but refuse to study their dialects, the languages in active use.

Language superiority is not an uncommon sentiment but Arabs claim they have proof of the superiority of Arabic. First of all, Muslims believe the Koran, which is written in classical Arabic, came directly from God. Classical Arabic, being the medium through which God chose to communicate must therefore be superior to all other languages. They further claim its complex grammar lends itself to rhythm and rhyme, making it aesthetically pleasing to listen to when recited aloud.

TAKING LESSONS

Even though learning Arabic is difficult, it will certainly help you gain insight into the society and culture. The Arabs will be pleased and will regard you highly for trying and may even view you as something of a scholar. When taking lessons from Arabs, they will want to teach you classical Arabic because that is what, in their opinion, scholars study. The people I have known to attempt lessons in the Emirates usually quit in frustration when they are unable to convince their teachers to teach them the local dialect. You must be highly motivated to learn the language in order to overcome the obstacles mentioned. Arabs are extremely flattered by efforts to learn their language. Your efforts, no matter how poor, will be met with appreciation and delight.

Many Arabic expressions make reference to God and sound flowery when translated literally into English. They are commonly used in Arabic by foreigners in the Emirates even amongst each other.

LANGUAGE NEED

Language learning is greatly facilitated by need and the biggest obstacle to learning Arabic in the UAE is that there is simply very little need for the English speaker to speak and understand Arabic. The Arabic that is needed tends to be suited to situations and includes a smattering of Urdu. Such situations tend to present themselves in taxis and shops that cater primarily to Arabs, where the shopkeeper is less likely to know English.

Some Arabic words having cultural or religious value are used hundreds of times a day. These are *In sha'Allah* (God willing), *Mafi mooshcola* (It is no problem), and *Al hamdu lilah* (Thanks be to God). No matter how little of the language one does learn, these expressions become automatic for everyone. These expressions can be annoying particularly *In sha'Allah* because it is said every time reference is made to the future. To the foreigner it feels like someone is saying, "Maybe, maybe not" when actually the Emirati means to agree that the event will happen but that it is entirely up to God. This leaves some degree of uncertainty and even suggests impropriety in being exact about the future.

Along the lines of annoying situations are ritualistic greetings which can last a very long time. These are especially annoying when they interrupt your very important business. An Emirati will answer the telephone or greet a friend or second customer as they enter the shop even though you may be speaking. Much patience is called for from those accustomed to giving and receiving undivided attention from an early age, and who must realise that the Arab has learned to participate in several conversations at once. The more you can participate in these interruptions (i.e. greeting the newcomer) and understand that they are not personal snubs aimed at you, the easier it will be for you to go about your business.

THE PLACE OF ENGLISH

The Emiratis have realised their need to learn English. Dubai, being a major trading port, deals with people from all over the world and the Emiratis there must communicate in English. Abu Dhabi is the home of the government and sees ambassadors, diplomats, and official visitors from all over the world. These people have learned to communicate across their varied backgrounds through English. Both cities sell most of their oil to Western, English speaking countries. The country's white collar workers all tend to be English speakers and communicate with each other in the language that is most comfortable to them – English. Even the Emirati policeman who responds to the scene of an accident may be faced with two English speaking drivers and be frustrated if he cannot speak a common language with them.

The Emiratis study English from grade school through college. They have great difficulty learning English because of the great differences in the writing systems of the two languages. However, the Emiratis do realise the burden of language adjustment is on them. While writing in English is difficult for Emiratis, they learn to speak

English with relative ease and clarity. A lengthy oral tradition may contribute to their verbal linguistic adeptness.

ARABIC AND THE KORAN

Because Arabic is the language of the Holy Koran, all Muslims, despite their nationality and location in the world, are at least a little familiar with it. People pay respect to written Arabic, believing that when no longer needed, script should be properly disposed of so that the name Allah and quotations from the Koran never have the chance of landing on the ground, where they might be stepped on or used to wrap things. Arabs even carry written blessings and verses from the Koran in silver necklaces specially made for this purpose. These serve to ward off the 'evil eye' brought on by such things as envious looks.

Korans are treated respectfully. They should be nicely displayed on the X-shaped wooden stands specifically made for this purpose or kept in their own velvet-lined boxes. One should never place anything on top of the Koran, place the Koran on the floor, or keep it with other common books.

A Koran open on a traditional stand. Jewellery containers for holding Koranic verses lie across the Koran.

ARABIC ART

Arabic art is almost never representational because Islam prohibits the representation of living things. Artists choose not to flout this tradition because they see reality as so beautiful, it would be futile to try and capture or copy it. Instead, Arabic art is decorative. This did not leave the Arabs many avenues in which to express themselves, so they became adept at constructing complex designs using plant patterns, geometric motifs, and Arabic script.

Arabic script uses twelve basic signs to write its 28 letters and these are then used with further variation to decorate objects such as bowls, dishes, book covers, door and window frames, and walls and domes of mosques. Verses from the Koran are usually the texts used in these pieces.

THE POWER OF WORDS

Arabs believe words have power, that words can affect the outcome of events. To ensure a good outcome, Arabs will interject blessings for good fortune. Conversely, they believe swearing and using obscenities will bring misfortune. They do not swear, curse or cuss and are alarmed when others do, because they believe the speaker will bring evil to them.

It follows that Arabs do not like to discuss anything bad such as illness or death since reference to bad things can make their outcome worse. Instead they use euphemisms, indirect expressions for something that might come across as harsh. The direct, honest approach favoured by some nationalities will shock the Emirati.

— *Chapter Nine* —

WOMEN IN THE EMIRATES

The Emirati women are the flowers of the desert. They are placed on pedestals and treated as reverently as precious jewels. Certainly subservient from a Western perspective but, from their own point of view, in dire need of protection, the women perpetuate their own role in this male dominated society in accordance with their cultural and religious beliefs.

LOYALTY AND LINEAGE

Members of a family show loyalty to each other through subservience and obedience to the best interests of the group. Family groups are led by a respected male figure who leads, guides and advises the members with wisdom and faith. Each member is loyal to all the other family members, including extended family. The greater the loyalty of the individuals, the more united a front the family presents. In return, the family protects its individual members.

A woman is always a member of her father's family. Even if she marries into another family, her loyalty is to the family she was born into. For this reason, she does not change her name when she marries. A woman's children are members of her husband's family. In a divorce, older children are automatically awarded to the father, unless special provisions have been made in the marriage contract. This works as a deterrent to divorce in cases where a woman does not wish to be separated from her children. However, the patrilineal descent can also work in a woman's favour. If a woman's husband or her husband's family mistreats her, she has her brothers and father at hand to rise up in her defence. When a woman's sons are old enough, they provide her with the support she received early in her marriage from her father and brothers.

Patrilineal descent strongly discourages marriage to members of other families or tribes. Women take strength and wealth in the form of children and inheritance away from their paternal families and to their husband's family when they marry someone outside the paternal family. A woman's offspring represent strength and increased numbers but belong to her husband. Her wealth passes to her children upon her death and thus, out of her father's family and into that of her husband. The ideal marriage then is one between the children of two brothers. Progeny of such a union can trace a common ancestor and wealth and strength are retained by the family. Awareness of the genetic problems engendered in the progeny of such unions is spreading but has not yet altered this value.

HONOUR

Individuals are loyal and responsible to the group they belong to before themselves. An individual's behaviour reflects back on the group and can bring shame and dishonour or glory and honour. Pressure to maintain good standing within the group is strong enough to deter most people from behaving in ways that would exclude them from their group. In the past, people who were tossed out of the group had no choice but to wander around the desert. This meant certain death. Even if wanderers came upon other groups, those groups would provide them with the obligatory three days of hospitality but not with group membership.

When individuals did bring shame and dishonour to their group through their misconduct, the group had to restore its honour. The only way a group could restore its honour was to punish the guilty individual. The greatest dishonour a group could experience was brought about through the sexual misconduct of one of its female members. These rules still hold true today. Thus, every aspect of Emirati society, from segregation and veiling, to being escorted and homebound, offers women protection from the possible loss of their honour. Women, recognising the value of their virtue, see these practices as providing them with protection and are in favour of retaining them.

A woman who commits adultery will be punished by her father and brothers on whom she has brought shame. Capital punishment, the sentence for adultery, is rarely meted, since four witnesses to the crime are required to carry the punishment out. Where four witnesses cannot be found, the woman will receive 100 lashes. The husband is responsible for seeking revenge from the woman's lover who has impinged on his property rights. Revenge is achieved by killing the wife's lover. However, the husband has not suffered the dishonour her family has because she is a member of her father's family, not her husband's. The woman's family may regain face through punishing her, but the woman's honour is lost and can never be regained.

A woman's honour can be lost rather easily through a tarnished reputation. A friend of mine attended the woman's half of a wedding celebration. She was in a tent with 15 young, unmarried Emirati women between the ages of about 16 and 25. They were dancing wildly to an upbeat modern Arabic tune, gyrating their hips passionately in an effort to outdo each other. At a word from one of the older girls watching at a flap in the tent, the girls dove for their discarded veils, covering every inch of skin, every dazzling jewel, and every last stitch of embroidery. Breathlessly they began conversing in hushed tones and giggles as five older women marched into the tent. The women stayed about a half hour, eyes darting about behind their masks, sizing up each of the young women present. The talk continued in hushed tones after the women had gone but gradually grew more and more lively until the dancing began again. This same scenario played itself out several times throughout the evening. My friend asked why the girls stopped dancing when the older women came in the room and was told the old women, essentially the matchmakers, would think they were loose and spoil their reputations. So the whole scenario was a challenge, as are the tame (by Western standards) sideways glances across the market place and the daringly bared ankles. Too much of it though, and word gets around.

CONDUCT IN PUBLIC

Emirati women are usually escorted by a close male relative when in public. Some of them have trusted drivers to take them to specific destinations. These drivers may be servants who have been with the family for many years and have earned a loyalty and trust akin to that reserved for family members. Women may also be seen in groups at the shopping centres. They are never alone in public. Women alone in public appear morally lax to the Emiratis.

Men and women do not display affection in public. They do not hold hands or touch in any way. While many Western behaviours, such as immodest dress and dating, are tolerated, touching between men and women in public is not. People are not arrested but they may receive a tirade of Arabic abuse from offended passers-by.

In the past, Emirati women did not eat in front of strangers. This was because eating required the lifting of veils. This practice has relaxed with the availability of private rooms and family rooms where the strangers are almost all women. They did not use public toilets. Instead, they waited all day until sunset and went for a collective walk to take care of that business. This practice too has become more relaxed and separate facilities for men and women greatly assist matters of decorum.

WEALTH

Women have the right to own property. They acquire their wealth through inheritance. The Koran says a woman is entitled to inherit half as much as her male siblings. A woman also acquires wealth in the form of gifts when she marries. These gifts are bestowed on her by the husband and his family and include many things, such as gold and precious jewels. In fact, women store their wealth in their jewels and wear them every day without the least bit of self-consciousness.

Women have complete ownership of their wealth and they do not contribute to household expenditures. Men are expected to provide complete material welfare for the upkeep of the house, yet household purchasing decisions are usually made by the wives, as are decisions as to how to raise and educate children and whom the children should marry. Women who actually use their wealth to further it or enter into business are few. Most defer to the wishes or advice of close male relatives or don't do anything with it at all. Some wealthy widows may hire an agent to conduct their business. This gives them freedom to do as they please through a male puppet voice.

STATUS OF WOMEN

Before the Prophet Mohammed began preaching the teachings of Allah, women truly did hold a subordinate position in Arab society. Islam is mistakenly thought to have lowered the status of women when in fact it raised their status, through granting them rights for the first time.

Women no longer had to marry their cousins, but were allowed to marry any men who were believers. The Koran states that a woman's dowry is to be given to her and not to her family. Thus, she may truly own her own wealth. It became illegal for a man to divorce his wife on false charges, and punishment for extramarital affairs became equally as wrong and punishable for men as it had been for women. Women were given the right to inherit and even though this amount is half as much as a man will inherit, it is 100% more than in pre-Islamic times. Infanticide was made illegal and this largely increased the survival rate for female babies. Development of the role and status of women since has been slow in the Gulf because the area has been isolated from much of the developed world up until about the last 20 years. However, because of the high status of Emirati women in the Emirates, and strong support from the government, the UAE women should be able to strengthen their position in society with relative speed and ease.

Men and women are considered to be equal in God's eyes. According to Emirati belief, people should be measured by their piousness and devotion to their religion rather than by their skin colour or gender. Thus, holding women in subordinate roles has been due to traditional institutions and their resistance to change more than to Islam.

EMIRATI WORKING WOMEN

Long ago, women had considerably more freedom to move about the village and they did work. They assisted their fathers and brothers with the herds, fetched water from wells, and went to market to buy and sell food. Then slaves were brought to the region and the wealthy began to distinguish themselves by covering their faces and sending the slaves out to do the work. Labourers now do the work once done by slaves.

Statistics in the Arab world in regard to women are unreliable, so it is difficult to say how many are actually in the workforce now,

Emirati women buying groceries at the local market.

particularly because most of those are not visible to the public. Emirati women have only had the right to work, in a modern day sense, for the past 10–20 years. Only a handful of women exercise this right and they do so through the permission of their male relatives. Emirati women who do work are found in schools, banks, hospitals and a few public utilities offices. These are all fairly reserved places where interaction can be controlled and women are treated with respect.

Women have greater access to high-level executive positions in the Emirates than women in other countries because the country has a need for more Emirati leaders and because women are kept out of the public eye in these positions. Where strange men come and go, as in banks and public offices, women are provided a private room or a wall with a hole for speaking and passing papers and money through. They are treated respectfully by customers and co-workers alike. At the hint of scandal or the diminishing of their reputation in any way, they are removed and not replaced.

Traditional beliefs, familial responsibilities and feelings of prestige hinder women from reaching work related goals. For example, there are not yet any fully practising female doctors. Family responsibilities or the difficulty of the internship keep bringing their careers to an end. A handful of women are getting close to completion though. Some Emirati women have tried nursing, but often they quit when they find it is not unlike being a servant, a position beneath them. Jobs such as sales clerk or hotel receptionist are also not suitable because they are considered to be putting women on public display. As long as these attitudes prevail, the Emiratis will continue to be dependent on expatriate workers to fill these types of positions.

Working women earn equal pay and time off for equal hours worked. They are given maternity and parenting leave and are paid their salaries when they take leave. A Muslim woman is required to mourn in complete seclusion for four months and ten days when her husband dies. The government has legislated her job be held for her and her salary be paid to her during this period in order to encourage her to remain in the workforce.

Money is not usually an issue, most Emirati women do not have a financial need to work. However, the Emiratis realise a need to increase their national workforce and are slowly trying to introduce their women to the workplace. The hurdle they must overcome is bringing about societal acceptance and that is slow and often backsliding.

An example of how introducing new customs to the society works lies in education. In 1977, the Emirates opened a university and a separate women's campus and facilities were provided for in Al-Ain. The number of women attending the university remained around a few hundred for years. These women were provided with on-campus housing with an imposing wall around the campus and guards at the gates. They were restricted from coming and going just as they would be at home. A few parents felt comfortable enough with the situation to allow them to attend. Society waited with discouraging frowns for the outcome of such a daring step. When young women graduated without scandal, a few more families allowed their daughters to attend. Enrolment has steadily increased ever since. In the past few years, enrolment has been doubling annually indicating ever increasing if not total societal acceptance.

Accepting women in the workplace is more difficult because it is not as easy to safeguard reputations in public. Even where a woman is provided a private room to assist female customers, there are times when she must communicate with male colleagues. In a lot of cases, an acceptable solution has not yet been found. The most backward and conservative of Emirati Muslims see a woman's role as that of domestic supervisor, responsible for raising children and providing sexual pleasure. More forward thinkers believe women should be educated, allowed to work and trusted with making decisions. They remember back to the days when people lived in small villages and women were seen in public and had social freedom because of the safe environment. The greatest concern of both the conservative and the liberal thinkers is the protection of a woman's virtue. They are currently figuring out how to enable women to have greater equality in light of their beliefs.

WESTERN WORKING WOMEN

Surprisingly, professional women will find themselves treated with an equality and respect at work as yet unknown in many countries. Colleagues, male and female, take their opinions seriously and women are as likely to be promoted as men. Equal compensation is even made for comparable work. The Emirates are a veritable paradise for women seeking an equal voice and equal opportunities at work.

Having a population of barely two million gives women (everyone for that matter) the opportunity to start businesses or other endeavours they always dreamed of. Thus, Western women are often active in starting businesses, professional organisations and clubs. In the Emirates, the time, funds and facilities are available to achieve such goals.

Secretarial and retail positions are often subject to the same discrimination, harassment, tedium, and lack of respect as they are in the home country. They might be a little more interesting in the Emirates because of the cultural variety. However, this may cause them to be more frustrating as well. While these positions do pay a little better than they would at home, the cost of living in the Emirates is significantly higher.

RESPONSIBILITIES

Women uphold traditions and customs by practising them in the home and passing them on to their children. They are encouraged in this respect through societal pressures. The behaviour of children reflects back on the success of a woman in her role as mother and a husband's praise and admiration of her in this role come as welcome rewards.

A wife manages affairs concerning the home and family. She decides how her children will be educated and whom they should marry. She provides her children with all the emotional support they need in order for them to depend on her, in fact, most children align themselves with their mothers their whole lives.

A wife budgets all home expenses. While this is more often a matter of deciding what to spend money on, rather than how far the budget will stretch, Emiratis are differently consumeristic from other newly wealthy groups of people. Their homes remain fairly devoid of furniture, wall-hangings, and knick-knacks. They still sit on the floor when eating and entertaining and gifts given and received are either food, flowers or jewellery, that is, things eaten or worn or having a short life span but not displayed. When making purchases, the value of money tends not to come into play. They purchase the things they see and like, bargaining more out of habit than necessity or budget consciousness. Shopkeepers know this and assign three prices to their merchandise: the Emirati or tourist price (exorbitant); the Western price (reasonable or slightly higher); and the working man's price (very reasonable with only a slight profit).

The wife also supervises the servants of which there may be many. Servants cook, drive their employers to school and the market, clean the house and take care of the children. Most households have at least one live-in servant, others have more servants than family members. Stories make the rounds among the Emiratis of children who are raised almost exclusively by servants and speak Tagalog or Hindi better than Arabic. There may be such cases but it is more likely the rumours have been embellished to encourage women to be more attentive mothers.

As for a wife's conjugal duties, they are not usually considered duties but rather privileges of marriage. Sex is encouraged within a marriage in this society. An Emirati's sex life is as normal or abnormal and varied as any. However, a couple's sex life is considered to be a very private matter and will never even be alluded to. In fact, enquiring about the health of a man's wife is a grave offence as it implies the woman is loose. None of this is to say the topic of sex is not discussed, it is and at length. Children learn all they ever need to know in the majlis where the women discuss the general topic quite descriptively without ever making reference to personal experience.

Finally, the wife is responsible for attending to the guests. For male guests she is behind the scenes directing servants in the kitchen and making sure the feast is lavish enough and well presented. With her female guests, her manners are impeccable because she herself has been taught well. She rises when anyone other than a servant or child enters a room, she says hello and welcome repeatedly and asks about her guests comfort throughout a visit. She gives her guests the seat of honour and encourages them to eat endless amounts of food, while eating little herself. She is a confident and excellent hostess, always remaining dignified and in good humour.

PASSING THE TIME

Emirati women devote hours to attending to beauty, from applying henna to their hands and feet and paying visits to beauty salons, to having their nails manicured and their hair treated with oils. Sadly, exercise is not part of the beauty regime. In fact, movement is avoided whenever possible. Large, soft women are beautiful to the Emiratis. Heavy-set foreigners are often more comfortable in the Middle East in general because it is a place where they can feel beautiful and desirable, an escape from the reed-thin ideal in other countries. However, great obesity falls outside the realm of desirability. It is not true that the size of a man's wife reflects his wealth. Number of wives rather than size is a more accurate indicator.

When not entertaining guests or primping, Emirati women are shopping. Endless hours are devoted to purchasing shoes and jewellery and to visiting tailors for the purpose of having numerous dresses made. It is amazing what a good fit a tailor can achieve never having measured the woman for whom he has made a dress. Shopping efforts are stepped up for special occasions such as Ramadan and weddings, when wardrobes must be entirely revamped. It seems a bit excessive when they just cover themselves in black scarves, but the Koran advises them to dress well albeit discreetly. Nor is their effort wasted. How well they dress reflects their status and once they arrive at a function, their veils are removed and their female relatives see them and form, or reinforce already formed opinions of them.

Not all Emirati women are lithe and graceful. Some look as awkward in their lovely gowns as if they were wearing them for the first time. Not all the women are beautiful either. Some are shy, while some are outgoing and some are self-confident but others are not. There is as much variety in personality and appearance with them as there is in any culture. However, two characteristics that do abound are hospitality and virtue.

Chapter Ten

RELIGION

BOUNTIES ARE FROM GOD

Religion and daily life are practically synonymous in the Emirates. Religion informs behaviour and is interspersed in the language through frequent expressions making reference to God. Religious practices may feel invasive the way they are widely and publicly practised. For example, prayer call will wake you every morning between 4:30 and 5:00; government workers will disappear in the middle of a transaction to pray; and the attempt to get a commitment to a future obligation will be placed in God's hands. The more you understand the Emiratis' religion, the more tolerant you will be of those things that are invasive. You will also be less likely to cause offence yourself.

Close to 100% of the Emiratis are of the Sunni Muslim sect. Islam means submission to the will of God and a Muslim is one who submits. Islam guides every aspect of the Emiratis' lives. Care must be taken to avoid causing offence by saying or acting in ways that go against Islam. This becomes easier in a very short time once you become accustomed to societal norms. Emiratis are amazingly tolerant of other religions (with the exception of Judaism, discussed later in this chapter). They respect the beliefs others hold and are impressed by religious devotion. They do not, however, comprehend a lack of religious faith. So while Emiratis may curiously interrogate you about your beliefs, if you are atheist or agnostic, keep it to yourself. They don't understand and may express shock at such a declaration.

Expressing an interest in Islam is always appreciated. Emiratis know quite a bit about Christianity and are amazed at how little Christians know about Islam. They are happy to educate the uninformed and an information exchange may turn into an attempted conversion. It is well meant. The Emiratis love their religion and God. Their enthusiasm and religious fervour is overflowing. They are still concerned about not offending you though and may feel badly if their enthusiasm causes you discomfort. Their tolerance of you and desire to make you comfortable inform their face to face interactions with you, it is only fair that you reciprocate.

SIMILARITIES BETWEEN ISLAM AND CHRISTIANITY

Muslims view their religion as a continuation of Christianity, but see Islam as the one true faith. The reason Islam is viewed as a continuation of Christianity is due to the significant similarities between the two religions. They share the concept of a Heaven and a Hell with a Satan figure presiding over Hell and God (Allah) in Heaven. Muslims and Christians believe that on the final day when God judges mankind, each person will receive their just reward or punishment as they deserve, based on the way they lived their life. Followers of both religions recognise many prophets in the histories of their religions, many of whom are the same for both religions. These prophets had repeatedly to teach the people through the centuries because the people continually strayed from their teachings.

People of each faith, Christian and Muslim, believe only the doctrines of their faith are true and valid. They believe that there is little hope for those who have heard the doctrine and do not believe. For the Emiratis, the more they like you, the more they may try to convert you because they are deeply concerned about your prospects for meeting God in the end.

AND A FEW DIFFERENCES

Muslims believe as Christians do that Jesus was born of the Virgin Mary (Miriam in Arabic) and that he performed miracles. They believe as Christians do that he raised the dead, fed the poor, and cured the sick. Where they differ in their belief, and this is pivotal, is that they see Jesus as a prophet and not as the son of God. Muslims do not believe Jesus was crucified but that it was someone else who died on the cross. Christians believe in a holy trinity of God, his son Jesus, and the holy spirit. Muslims believe there is only God. Thus, while Christians can pray to Jesus to intercede with God on their behalf, Muslims pray directly to God only. Emiratis are particularly curious about this point and if you are interested in taking on the argument, you will need to be well read and knowledgeable or else risk losing face. If you would prefer not to be engaged in a religious debate, state that you do not care to discuss your religious beliefs.

In the West, Church and state have pretty well been separated. This is not the case in the Emirates where religion is the source of law and not long ago was even the sole resource for educators. Muslims do not wish for any reduction of the role of religion in their lives.

PARADISE

Muslims are very focused on the afterlife. They believe they will go to a paradise with lush gardens, tall green trees, and flowing waters. In many ways they try to create that paradise here on earth. Al-Ain, the garden city of the Emirates, is heavily watered to ensure palm trees will grow throughout the city. Palm trees do indeed grow, serving the purpose of providing shade and keeping the sand out of the city centre at least. It becomes hard to comprehend how a country fast running out of fresh water and depleting its water table daily could continue to water this vision of paradise, but there it is.

THE FIVE PILLARS OF ISLAM

The five pillars of Islam are the main rules Muslims follow in their lifetimes. These pillars are the profession of faith, prayer, fasting, alms-giving, and a pilgrimage to Mecca. The first pillar, the Declaration of Faith, states, "There is no God but God and Mohammed is the messenger of God." This is the declaration made when professing faith or converting to Islam. When converting to Islam, the declaration must be made in front of two male Muslims.

The second pillar is prayer five times a day. These prayers are said at dawn *(salat al fajr)*, noon *(salat al bohor)*, afternoon *(salat al 'asar)*, sunset *(salat al-maghrib)* and at night *(salat al leela)*. Their timing varies every day in connection with the rising and setting of the sun. Prayers are said to pay respect to God and to give him thanks. Muslims are notified of prayer time by a call broadcast from loud-speakers at the top of mosques. There are plenty of mosques in the Emirates so all can hear and heed the call. Prior to praying, Muslims wash themselves in order to be ritually purified in preparation for prayer. Muslims can pray anywhere, inside, outside, even in another country but they must face Kaaba in Mecca as they pray. They rise and prostrate themselves several times during the prayer. The number of times a worshipper rises and prostrates is different for each of the five prayers.

Jumairah Mosque – the number of mosques make it possible for every male Muslim to attend prayer calls and services.

The third pillar is giving alms to the needy. Muslims are required to give a percentage of their goods or earnings to the welfare of the community and also to the poor. In the Emirates, food is distributed once a week at palace gates to the needy who come for it. It is very unlikely you will see a beggar in the Emirates, but if you do, you should give something even if it is only a few coins. If you do not have those, then say *Allah yateek* meaning "May God give you." In so doing, you have at least given a blessing.

The fourth pillar requires Muslims fast during Ramadan. A fasting Muslim takes neither food nor drink, not even water, between sunrise and sunset. Smoking is also prohibited. Fasting causes the Muslim to know hunger and deprivation and many are humbled by the experience. This act of self-discipline is an expression of faith. For more information on Ramadan, see the section at the end of this chapter.

The fifth pillar requires Muslims perform a pilgrimage to Mecca at least once during their lifetime if it is not a financial hardship. Mecca is located in Saudi Arabia and is one of the holy cities. This pilgrimage is known as the *Hajj* and is the height of religious experiences for Muslims. The Hajj is performed in the 12th month of the Islamic year. Muslims from all over the world come to Mecca and carry out worship activities and rituals at different holy sites there over a period of six days. These activities and rituals end with the sacrificing of a sheep by those who can afford it. They share their feast with those who cannot. Single women are not permitted to enter Saudi Arabia, so they are not expected to satisfy the fifth pillar.

PRAYER

Prayer is very important to Emiratis, but prayer practices are not as extreme as they are reported to be in Saudi Arabia. There is no public criticism of people who choose not to pray. Stores and businesses are not expected to close during prayer time but the man assisting you may disappear for a short while, leaving you alone in his shop or else his assistant might help you and then take his turn to go to the mosque.

There is supposed to be a mosque within five minutes walking distance of every male Muslim. There are an amazing number of mosques in the Emirates and it would not be a surprise if this goal has already been reached. Most men do not get to the mosque for every prayer, but they do try to make it at least once a day. Friday noon is the most important prayer of the week and political speeches are given along with the usual religious messages.

Women usually pray at home though Abu Dhabi and Dubai do have mosques for women only. Other religions hold their usual main services on Friday and a smaller one on Sunday for those who can make it. Friday is the one day a week when everyone has the day off.

RAMADAN

Ramadan, the month of fasting, takes place during the ninth month of the Islamic calendar. Because of the difference between the Islamic calendar and the Gregorian one, Ramadan occurs about two weeks earlier every year. Ramadan is the time when God revealed the Koran to the prophet Mohammed. Muslims are supposed to focus their spiritual growth and development during this month through increased prayer, meditation and observance of religious practices.

Ramadan is looked forward to with great anticipation. The month prior to Ramadan has a festive, holiday atmosphere to it. It is called *Sha'ban*, the time to make preparations. Emiratis and other Muslims redecorate their homes to prepare for visits from family, friends and neighbours. Many new clothes are made for the Emiratis by local tailors who work long, hard hours to complete the orders. It is a good idea to postpone trips to a tailor until after Ramadan when having a new outfit made. Emiratis purchase large amounts of goods such as pillows and carpets to sit on and mattresses for their many anticipated overnight guests. Large amounts of food are also purchased, especially staples. Emiratis keep plenty of snacks on hand, dates and nuts are particularly popular. All this shopping greatly eases the chore during Ramadan when people are too hungry to attend to it. Shops are open late during Ramadan to meet the schedule needs of people fasting. The souks hum with life and a walk through them will allow you to witness the holiday spirit during the night, when the temperature is cooler.

People also prepare for Ramadan during the month of Sha'ban by resolving conflicts they are having with others. They finish large projects and diminish their work load. This enables them to purify themselves and enter into the spirituality of Ramadan without distraction. Women have special preparations since they can anticipate being 'unclean' and therefore unable to participate in the fasting for part of Ramadan. This unclean time is a woman's period. She is prohibited from fasting as are pregnant women, those in poor health, and young children. Women must make up the missed time either before or after Ramadan. Those in poor health must make up the missed time when they are able. People who travel should not fast and are also required to make up the missed time.

Many Emiratis attempt to read the entire Koran during the month of Ramadan. This does not leave them much time for other academic pursuits. Ramadan does not excuse a Muslim from his or her duties, however in reality, school and work hours are reduced and less is expected because people slow mentally and physically from the effects of fasting as the month continues. Evening prayer services are held nightly and special hours are set aside for women. It is the one month of the year when women regularly attend the mosque

Work hours are shorter during Ramadan than they are during the rest of the year. Work hours change so that most work is done in the early morning or late at night after the fast has been broken. This evening meal is called *iftar* and is often followed by a very late night/ early morning second meal (breakfast) called *suhur*. The Ramadan schedule can be quite intrusive if you live in apartment housing that has shops on the bottom floors. Work may continue through the night in those shops and be closed during the day. There is not much you can do about the disturbance because Ramadan takes precedence over your needs.

While you will not be expected to fast, it is illegal for you to be seen eating, drinking or smoking in public between sunrise and sunset. You should be careful even in the privacy of your own home not to eat or drink in front of a Muslim. It is very rude to tempt someone focused on improving their spirituality. Fasting brings on somewhat of a religious fervour, a euphoria. People feel very close to God and in tune with their beliefs. In 'The Gulf playground' this results in less tolerance of Western vices. All restaurants are closed until evening prayer call is heard. Bars are closed for the month, instead, hotels open shop in their larger suites. Because of the greater observance of religious practice, deviations from the law are less tolerable during this month.

Tempers get shorter as the month and the fast progress and your tolerance level may need to go up accordingly. Muslim scholars claim that the fast is beneficial in two ways. Physically the fast is supposed to cleanse the system. Spiritually it is beneficial for gaining greater control and discipline over the body's needs. You may wish to try the fast yourself to enter into the spirit of the season and to gain greater understanding of your hosts.

The spirit of Ramadan has gone a bit of the way of the spirit of Christmas in the West. Whereas what has already been said is technically accurate, Ramadan is also a big festival when people overindulge at night, and often spend large amounts of money on lavish gifts and banquets.

THE HOLY KORAN

The Koran contains the doctrines of Islam exactly as they were revealed to the prophet Mohammed. These revelations took place over a 22 year period. They explain correct behaviour for almost every aspect of a Muslim's life in order to attain salvation on the Final Judgement Day.

The Koran is mostly written in verse which is both cadenced and rhyming. Some of it is written in prose. Both lend themselves beautifully to recitation. In fact, the word 'Koran' means recitation. Those who can recite the entire Koran are bestowed the title *Hafiz* and are highly respected for their ability. Education in the past consisted solely of reciting the Koran. Memorisation of Koranic passages continues, but it no longer forms the entire educational curriculum.

The poetic quality of recited passages is truly beautiful. Emiratis and other Arabs take the aesthetic beauty of the Koran as proof of its being given to man by God. Emiratis have special jewellery they wear around their necks or, for men, on their dagger belts for holding favourite Koranic versus. These were ornate silver compartments in the past though now they are more likely to be made from gold. The older, tarnished and beaten up jewellery can be found in the souks and make popular souvenirs among tourists.

God revealed the Holy Koran to the prophet Mohammed in Arabic. Arabic is thus taken as the language standard in all Arab countries. Arabs value the ability to read and write the standard. Dialects, as different as they can be from the standard, are not written. Further, a translated version of the Koran may be used for study purposes, but not for prayer. So if you aspire to convert to Islam, it will be necessary for you to learn Arabic.

STRIFE OVER ISRAEL

Volumes have been written on this topic. Most accounts are biased in favour of one point of view or the other. This account is a simplified, unbiased and brief one to give you an overview of the issue.

Thousands of years ago, the Jews were driven out of their homeland and made slaves in Egypt. God promised to release them from slavery and after they wandered without a home for a very long time (generations), that He would deliver them to the promised land, Israel. When the Jews finally arrived in the promised land, Israel was occupied by Palestinians who did not recognise the Jewish claim to their land. The two groups have been fighting over Israel ever since. It is currently occupied by both the Jews and the Palestinians.

Governments of various countries have sided with one group or the other. The Emiratis do not support the Jewish occupation of Israel. They deal with the issue by denying it. On maps given to you, purchased or found at travel agencies, you will see that Israel has been marked out with a black marker. It was one of the topics I was not allowed to discuss in my classroom as if denying its existence will cause the problem to go away. As I mentioned previously, flights to Israel cannot be taken from or arranged in the Emirates and if you have an Israeli stamp in your passport, get a clean passport, you will not be issued a visa otherwise. If you are Jewish but hold a passport from a country other than Israel, you may be able to enter the country because your name may not make your religion apparent to the immigration officials.

The US often has an advisory against travelling to Israel and other Arab countries. This means they will probably not offer you assistance within the country if you are in danger or trouble because of political strife. Sometimes, however, the strife is viewed in a poorly understood or paranoid state by the West and you may wish to use your own discretion or the advice of recent travellers to your destination in making your travel decisions. Conflict among the Arabs, while frequent, is usually verbal, hence the endless peace talks between the different nations. Actual combat only occurs when things get out of hand and it is stopped as soon as possible. When CNN and the BBC are predicting imminent violent conflict in the Arab world, conflicts often do not result in physical violence and when they do they are usually short lived.

DJINN

Emiratis have a pre-Islamic belief in the supernatural which has survived the centuries. *Djinn* are spirits which can be either good or bad. They look very much like people and can even take the form of people we know. They have lives of their own and a society underground from which they occasionally arise. They live in the desert and are reluctant to enter the city. The Emiratis' pre-Islamic belief in them has survived and serves the purpose of explaining anything they do not easily understand. Emiratis claim the djinn can help or hurt people. Djinn are mentioned in the Koran which both provides people the greatest protection against them and lends them validity in the eyes of the Muslims.

Djinn are thought to appear most likely at dusk or dawn and people should be very careful at those times not to harm them by inadvertently stepping on them, riding over them or throwing something on them. The harmed djinn will repay the responsible party in kind. Of course, if one were dutifully at one's prayers, none of this would be a concern. Stories abound of encounters with djinn. You might be told one of these stories, but then again you might not because the Emiratis suspect you will not believe.

Chapter Eleven

DOING BUSINESS

BEYOND THE OIL BOOM

Growth resulting from increased oil production has stopped and the Emirates are maintaining their current output level. Even though the economy has slowed since the great oil boom, the Emirates are still in an expansion stage. For years I have been listening to foreigners predicting that the growth would have to stop soon, but it hasn't. Opportunities for doing business in the Emirates still abound. People are constantly coming and going, resulting in turnovers and vacancies. The service industry is ever expanding to support growth in the trade and construction businesses. Repair and maintenance work are lucrative businesses, because of shoddy workmanship up front and the harsh climate, and managers with education and experience are always in demand to oversee it all. However, the work is not increasing enough to create many new jobs so the competition is getting steeper.

SIMPLY THE BEST

The Emirates are on a superlative bandwagon. They boast the tallest building in the Middle East (Dubai Trade Centre); the world's largest man made port (Jebel Ali Port); the freest trade; and they are doing their best to attract big sports events – The PGA European circuit (golf) includes the greens of Dubai on its rounds, the 27th Chess Olympiad in 1986, and the annual Dubai Offshore Powerboat Race, to name a few.

The Emirates may only be in their mid 20s but they are sharp and quick to improve on new developments in the world. Japan was the bear in the international markets a few years ago, Korea is putting its tentacles out now, but the Emirates are using media hype to take the world by sudden storm. They purchase full page ads in foreign papers advertising their duty free shops and encouraging people to come and do business. They publish and market books with big colour photographs and flattering words about the country and they have cultural centres in foreign cities to further promote the country and culture. In 1992 when I mentioned to people where I was headed, they would ask, "Where exactly is that?" I almost never get that question any more.

ENVIRONMENT

While opportunities abound, no one is waiting for you to come and do them any favours. Getting your foot in the door is difficult when you don't know anybody. However, your climb may proceed faster and go further once you do get in if you are willing to put in the time on the job and if you adapt to their ways. Expect delays, frustrations and inconveniences and get the job done despite them. How? Be available and willing to work when there is work to be done. Most people in the business world always carry mobile phones and they're not reluctant to use them. A good attitude, acceptance of the local customs and conforming to their standards are keys to success.

INTERPERSONAL COMMUNICATION

Always consider a person's 'face' when communicating, including your own. Calm, controlled, unemotional or minimally emotional speech is most appropriate. Patience and quiet insistence may not move you any closer to your goal than will loud and forceful speech, but you will come out ahead in the future in not having lost respect among the Arabs. They may be more willing to say yes the next time.

Similarly, in dealing with an employee who is not meeting your expectations, compliment the employee on what he or she is doing well, enquire about the health of the employee and their family, and explain how you would like to see things done in the future. A more direct approach will surely be taken as a personal attack, cause the employee to lose face, and further encourage the behaviour in an opposite direction from which you had hoped to head. Do not ask an employee to do a job belonging to someone else and never reprimand an employee in front of other people.

Work is not an important topic of conversation with the Emiratis (though it probably is with foreigners). In fact, talking about work is pointless and perhaps a little silly, Emiratis think there are far better things to talk about, such as your good health and that of your family. Bedsides, the question would not be, "Who do you work for?" rather it would be, "What companies do you own?"

The Emiratis are open and sincere in communicating their wishes. While they do engage in ritualistic talk prior to discussing business, one does not have to decipher or second guess their meaning as they are inclined to state it directly. They look you in the eye when speaking and expect you to do the same. Looking down or away is interpreted as dishonesty. Emiratis may ask you a slew of questions you may consider to be personal. These may be about your family, age or income. It is important to them that you feel at ease, at home, a guest in their country and their business environment. Establishing a personal relationship with someone is a necessary precursor to establishing a business relationship. The more you warm up to them and they to you, the further your business will go.

'No' should be prefaced and softened, because saying it directly is offensive. You should be busy or offer some other reason why granting the request is not possible. Offer assistance at another time to further mitigate your refusal.

WORK ATTITUDES

Work attitudes are as varied as the population. People actually involved in business really do work hard. Expatriates in the private sector work a five and a half day week. Hours are long though, so for many people this usually equates to a six day work week. People who work for the government or ministries (usually Emiratis and diplomats) work a four and a half day week with rarely any overtime. Their jobs are secure and their attitude towards work is very relaxed compared to the small businessman who is trying to keep his company afloat.

Among the Emiratis, work attitudes also vary. The stereotypical Emirati businessman is government official, royalty, and sideline businessman all in one. He is so highly placed, all he does is attend one formal engagement after another. However, his less visible compatriot runs several businesses and is working as hard as anybody anywhere.

Work attitudes are much more relaxed in the Emirates than they are in many other countries. This is evidenced in the language. Ninety percent (my estimate and I'm being conservative) of utterances include, *Insha'allah* (God willing), *Ma'alish* (Don't worry), or *Mafi mooshcola* (No problem). These phrases are infuriating when it comes to your business and your deadlines. The only thing you can do about it is learn to be patient. I think one thing that helps is to look at life as one big picture, place your deadline in the picture and see how insignificant it is in comparison to the whole. Drink your tea, your business will be attended to in due time tomorrow, the day after or even, surprisingly, in the next few minutes.

Emiratis do not usually become overburdened by all their responsibilities as might be expected. Added responsibility does not increase the pace because there is always tomorrow to do the work, and if it doesn't get done, well that was God's will and out of the Emiratis control.

A carpet salesman busy relaxing between sales at an Emirati market.

WORK ENVIRONMENT AND ETIQUETTE

The Emirati businessman you need to talk to is probably busy. He may have several businesses of his own and serve as the chair for a half dozen or so committees and government offices. Other people need to see him too. Thus, his office will often be crowded and he will be conducting business with several people at once while signing official documents. All activity stops when a newcomer arrives (excepting the tea boy) and he is greeted by those already present. Anybody present can and will offer their own perspective on the business being discussed at any given moment. You may feel largely ignored, have patience, you will be attended to. If your business is sensitive, you may be asked to return at another time or be taken into another room and the door will be locked.

A busy associate may get down to business rather quickly, as he is too busy to spend much time coddling you. He will still ask ritualistic questions, just fewer of them and he will be less attentive to responses. Follow his lead and state your business when asked for it – clearly and succinctly, without leaving out important details. Avoid complicating your request.

Dirty Hands

A large percentage of the working population are adverse to doing anything outside of their job description, particularly if they feel it is beneath them. This is the 'dirty hands' concept and it is realised in a larger number of employees being required for work than might be necessary in other countries. Further, you would demean yourself in the eyes of others by doing work that is beneath your position. A hard worker who wants to start a business adopts the 'no dirty hands' concept with the public, then performs the work in private and realises a handsome profit. A private office is a sign of prestige. The importance of prestige cannot be overemphasised in a country where six of its seven leaders can boast of having an international airport and three of them a daily newspaper. As an owner, manager, or supervisor you will need your own office even if that is not your style. Psychologically, others will prefer to do business with such an important person as you, a person far removed from having dirty hands.

Doors are generally closed to keep in the air conditioning. Knock and enter. You will either be greeted by a receptionist who will announce you or enter a room full of people all waiting for their business to be attended to by the one man behind the big desk. Greet him, shake his hand, sit down as close to him as possible and have patience. He will probably attend to you fairly quickly out of curiosity if you are a Westerner since he sees few Westerners as compared to Middle and Far Easterners. Women usually do not have long to wait at all.

Men should always shake hands with other men when meeting them for the first time. A handshake should be short and firm. Your first question should be, "How are you?" followed by, "How is business?" and then, "How was your vacation?" or, "Did you have a nice weekend?" and anything else you can come up with of a not-too-personal nature. If a woman offers her hand, shake it, but don't put her in the awkward position of having to refuse your proffered hand because it is against her religious beliefs to touch you. In general, people accept that foreign women shake hands with men and women. However, I have been soundly rebuked for offering my hand to a Muslim man. The rules are pretty straightforward for men, but still in transition for women. Proceed with caution.

Manners and Dress

Emiratis see Westerners in particular as too liberal and sloppy about their appearance. The Emiratis in general are immaculate dressers. Their clothes are well pressed, and elegant in a subtly expensive way. Your dress reflects your status and wealth and you will be judged by your appearance. Your employers may even give you a dress code. Dress well – a couple of very nice, conservative outfits should suffice in the beginning.

Manners must be as impeccable as dress. The best mannered people get the job. These people are the ones who let the Emirati set the pace, follow his lead in introducing business and are sensitive to the amount of time the Emirati has or wants to devote to them. They wait for the Emirati to present his business card before offering theirs. Foreigners are forgiven most of their strange ways, particularly when their intentions are good. Openness needs to be tempered and subdued. If you cannot appear to be calm and relaxed, you should return when you are better able to master your feelings of anger and frustration or excitement and exuberance. Avoid insulting or shocking the Emiratis and try to be non-judgmental.

PERSONAL CONTACTS

Business success is most likely if you are personally around to conduct your business. Your physical presence is preferable to letters and faxes from home. Contacts are vital in doing business here, as they are in most places. Contacts will inform you of forthcoming projects before they are announced. Knowing the right people, and knowing and getting along with the Arabs, will ensure jobs go to you over other bidders. If you cannot be present yourself, you will need a representative or agent on a temporary (project) or permanent basis depending on your business.

As your business expands, the agent may appoint sub-agents or you may hire other agents for other emirates. Your agent, being the one with the contacts in the country, is in a better position to appoint other trusted and well connected people as agents than you are, so you are probably better off giving him the reins. Care needs to be taken in selecting an agent, because although removing them is theoretically possible, in reality they cannot be removed or changed once in place.

In a country where nepotism is prevalent, having established clout, or wasta, with a person in command, is your only way in. This clout results in greater efficiency in getting your work done and fewer stumbling blocks.

HIRE NATIONAL

As mentioned earlier, there is a concerted push to hire nationals over expatriates in government and business positions, when the positions are unrelated to manual labour. Contacts and wasta certainly assist in the hiring practice. Emirati men are assigned positions based on who they know. They often hold several government positions or commissions at one time.

Nepotism, while as widely practised as ever, has become less of a problem, now that most young nationals have good educations (many have college or university degrees and often those have been earned abroad) so it is likely that quality and productivity accompany the relative. Educated Emiratis have made it possible for the UAE to grow into a mature participant in the business world. With this maturity has come the desire and ability to take over business and development from foreigners.

BRIBES

While there is no tax, no Value Added or Goods and Services Tax, there are bribes. On the surface everything appears to be free, but in reality, a price is being paid. The contractors who bid for jobs may be beaten out by another company willing to bid extremely low and pay a kickback. It is acceptable practice to take a bribe but not for everyone to know about it. The trend is slowly moving away from this practice because when revealed it results in scandal. The government, which wields control over the economy as well as all aspects of society, has been so badly burned in some of these deals, that it is now forcing businesses to be more honest.

The combination of steep competition and behind the scenes bribes result in higher costs and corners needing to be cut. Corners may be cut on quality of supplies and labour, resulting in shoddy workmanship. This practice has benefited no one but the repair and maintenance industries.

CHAMBERS OF COMMERCE

Each emirate has its own customs and laws for doing business. Some of these laws contradict each other. Check with your embassy or the local chamber of commerce for guidance on doing business in your emirate. Do not assume the way you managed your affairs in Dubai will work twenty minutes away in Sharjah.

Each emirate has a chamber of commerce which organises the business of the community, such as awarding business licenses and settling inter-emirate business disputes. In the past this business and the business of the rulers of each of the seven emirates were one and the same. In the West, chambers of commerce tend to serve and inform the public or to advocate on behalf of individuals and small businesses. This is the ideal, as it serves common people rather than those in power. The chambers of commerce in the United Arab Emirates are slowly moving towards this ideal with a federal Economy and Commerce Ministry taking over the issuing of licenses and arbitrating disputes. Some changes are slow to take place in the Emirates, particularly those affecting the power of the rulers. While less political involvement is the goal, in reality, the chambers still largely serve the interests of the rulers.

LICENSES

Some licenses can only be obtained by nationals. Others can be obtained by foreigners who have a national for a partner or sponsor. The national is entitled to between 25% and 51% of the business depending on the type of license. Business agreements with UAE nationals tend to favour the nationals. However, there is a free zone called the Jebel Ali Free Zone, located between Dubai and Abu Dhabi, that was established to circumvent the requirement for national participation in foreign enterprise. Jebel Ali has a large port for goods to be shipped in and out. Special licenses, free of any national participation, can be obtained in this zone.

TAXES

There are no federal taxes in the Emirates as of yet, but each of the emirates may impose their own taxes. At this time, the Abu Dhabi government contributes the largest portion of tax revenue to the country, nearly 80%, Dubai contributes another 9% or so and the other emirates combined make up the remainder. Abu Dhabi, Dubai and Sharjah currently tax oil and banking businesses, while other small businesses and individuals are still free from paying taxes. These will very likely be forthcoming due to decreasing oil revenues.

ENTRY LEVEL

Entry level positions, such as secretary, office worker or shop keeper, are advertised in the newspapers. Agencies requesting and supplying temporary help dominate the want ads. These jobs do not usually offer benefits or a working visa and pay about dh5,000 a month (US$1,358), almost enough for a single person to live on. The ads do not mince words. They state exactly what they are looking for including gender, age, skin colour, accent and languages spoken.

Secretarial, office and shop staff jobs do not often come with opportunities for advancement anywhere and this is also true in the Emirates. There is a lot of lateral mobility at this level because employees change jobs when they receive a better offer. People who typically fill these positions are wives who don't have to worry about getting a work visa, Western women from GCC countries whose passports allow them to stay in the Emirates for 3–6 months without a visa, and people from poorer countries where salaries are much lower.

SALARIED EMPLOYEES

It is difficult to know ahead of time whether the salary and benefits package you are being offered will be competitive in the Emirates. You don't want to ruin your chances at a job by asking for more than the market offers, yet you will be disillusioned if you discover you have accepted a lower salary than your colleagues. You may feel you undersold yourself, while the Arab employer is feeling good about the bargain he got. Never mind that you may be a disgruntled employee and will cost him in turnover in the long run, he is pleased with his deal at the present time.

There are no set answers but a little advice will help one get on the right track. Get as much information as you can from prospective employers. If they are above board and reputable, they will supply you with satisfactory answers. Be careful, if a benefit you want is not in your contract, it will not be forthcoming after you arrive. If you want something, ask up front. One pitfall that may lead to job dissatisfaction is that while you will probably be given annual cost of living adjustments, raises are less likely. This is one way the Emiratis discourage people from staying in the country too long. If you are interested in annual reviews resulting in pay increases, you should get it in writing up front. I mentioned previously that a person's word is more important than a written contract. With large organisations, the contract will serve as the spoken word and with one's word goes honour so it will be followed.

Cost of Living

I can only give myself as an example. I lived on the frugal side of average on a salary of between dh7,000 and dh8,000 a month for three years, budgeting dh600 (US$160) a week as spending money. This paid for the upkeep of my car, my telephone bill and entertainment for myself. I did not have any other expenses since my house, furniture and utilities were paid for by my employer and I do not have children. I was able to save about US$10,000 a year and take trips through Europe, the Middle East and go home once a year. There are of course other professional occupations that pay considerably more than mine does and many service jobs that pay considerably less without providing the benefits I had.

You know best the salary range for your field in your home country. While you can expect a higher salary and better benefits in the Emirates, you will also need to budget in the higher cost of living. People often find the free education their children received back home takes a big chunk of their budget in the Emirates. A night out also costs considerably more than back home, perhaps twice as much and people tend to go out much more often when they live overseas. Things you will want to negotiate in advance are: shipping, medical insurance, housing, a furniture allowance, education for children, round trip airfare, a transportation allowance, and an annual repatriation ticket. Many of these fringe benefits are inclusive in offers from well established, knowledgeable employers, but do not take any of them for granted. Get agreements in writing when negotiating a contract.

SMALL BUSINESS OWNERS

Foreigners in business for themselves are usually involved in the import/export business or are professionals in independent practice. With a few exceptions (discussed under Licenses), business owners are required to have a national as a sponsor or business partner. Oil and gas exports account for the largest portion of the export business, an estimated 75%. However, the UAE is also a place to buy products reasonably cheap and to resell them at home for 150 to 200 times as much. These products come from Japan, South Korea, China, Britain, and the US and are re-exported at profit. The re-export trade has existed in the Emirates since traders first began landing their boats on the coast. Opportunities for making money in the re-export business constantly shift with global political and economic conditions. Currently the Russians are shipping electronics out like mad. It is actually astonishing to behold. Perhaps a dozen people fly in on a full size aircraft that only has about a dozen seats. These dozen shop and play for a week or only a weekend, load their goods aboard a similar craft carved out to hold the goods and a few passengers, and head home to sell their wares to a middle man. Many ports around the world can complain about the same phenomena at this time, but it is doubtful whether any are so blatantly obvious as the ports in Dubai and Sharjah.

There is supposed to be a tariff on goods in the Emirates, but over half the goods come in and go out duty free. Things that are watched more closely and that are definitely taxed are alcohol, weapons and chemical substances. Alcohol and tobacco products are taxed at 30%. Drugs, pornography, and anti-Islamic literature are entirely illegal.

Professionals in business for themselves are medical doctors, psychiatrists, psychologists, dentists, lawyers, and others whose services cannot be 'stolen' from them. They have a national as a sponsor or business partner as it is required by law. They are unique in their professions in that they need to be familiar with the Arab culture and language. Financially, they do well. (Imagine a lawyer's salary – tax free!)

Small business owners in the Emirates are able to benefit from the tax free environment and liberal trading regulations.

181

EXPECTATIONS

Are you able to cope with a new culture, a new job and an entirely new social life all at the same time? Are you willing to? Is your family? To assist you and your family, learn as much as you can about the local customs. Know the standard of education your children will be receiving and know too that the high quality of education your children received back home may not be available to them in the Emirates and if it is, it is probably extremely expensive. Consider the current cost of living, compare it to your own at home, so you are prepared for the out of pocket expenses you may encounter. Learn as much as you can about your employer, how long he has been in business, how lucrative his business is or else who is funding the business. If a sheikh is funding it, it will be around as long as the sheikh wishes it to be and not longer. Find out about your work conditions – air conditioning, crowded, on-site, etc. and your responsibilities.

OPPORTUNITIES

Those coming to set up businesses should know that any raw materials they need in developing a product will have to be imported and the product itself will have to be exported because the local market is shrinking due to increased competition and a steady or even contracting population. You must also factor in the cost of skilled local labour, which is expensive. However, if your business requires a lot of energy, it comes cheaply through gas and the Emiratis are often willing to put forth capital, and award large tax breaks.

Light industry, those industries which add value to existing products, can avail themselves of low cost energy and a skilled workforce. The most modern communications technology assists them in doing business internationally and an excellent infrastructure keeps business moving internally. The Emirates provide a perfect environment for specific businesses able to avail themselves of the resources the country has to offer, other businesses should think twice before jumping into a very competitive market.

CULTURAL QUIZ

Now that you have read the book try these quiz questions to test your knowledge of how best to react in certain situations. Life in the Emirates can be a rewarding experience for those willing to take the time and effort to understand the Emiratis and their culture. The best advice to anyone confronted with a new culture is to conduct yourself with respect and courtesy, your mistakes and indiscretions will usually be overlooked until you have become more comfortable with your new environment.

This book will provide a useful springboard in helping you to cope during the early stages of your life in the Emirates. Use it in conjunction with your own experiences and your time in the UAE will be as much an education as a period of employment.

SITUATION ONE

Your Emirati employer has invited you to a lavish feast at a five-star hotel. You arrive to find lots to drink, discreet waiters and only two other women. One is a Westerner enjoying herself immensely, the other is a scantily clad Russian dancer putting on a show for five leering men. What do you do?

A Relax and enjoy yourself. Your employer is simply letting his hair down, showing you he can accept and enjoy your ways too.

B Politely greet everyone and ask to speak to your employer in private. Let your employer know that you did not realise the nature of his invitation and that you do not feel comfortable participating.

C Join the festivities but find an excuse to leave soon, such as becoming suddenly ill.

Comments

You may opt for any of the above and everyone decides differently for themselves. The problem with A is that your employer is flouting his own traditions and beliefs. His behaviour is not acceptable or legal but some Emiratis believe God cannot see them when they are not on holy ground. A Western hotel is certainly not seen as holy ground. While he may enjoy your 'ways,' he does not accept them or respect you for them.

Answer C will solve your problem in the situation but you will be invited to such occasions again and again. Eventually, you are going to need to go with option B. You will begin to recognise these invitations when they are initially made so you can avoid them before you are faced with them. If you opt to participate in them, your reputation will suffer.

There is little that is not known by everyone in such a small place and it becomes difficult to know whom to trust when everyone is talking behind your back. Also, you must think about what kind of a relationship you want with your employer. The more professional it is, the less trouble and conflict you will have. If your employer is inviting you to an occasion involving the women of his family, you are very fortunate and should take advantage of such a privilege without having to fear for your reputation.

SITUATION TWO

Upon returning from an extended vacation, you run into one of your well educated Emirati friends. She informs you she married while you were gone. You express delight and ask her whom she has married. "You mean his name, miss?" she enquires with some dubiousness as to how you could possibly expect to know him. "No," you say, "I mean is he your cousin?" "No!" she exclaims knowing full well cousin marriage is unacceptable in a modern society, "He is my mother's, sister's son," she explains. What do you say?

A Explain the blood relationship is the same on the mother's side as it is on the father's.

B Congratulate her and wish her well.

C Express an interest in this new event in her life, question her about how she likes being married, what her new husband is like, and how life is different for her now.

Comments

A will bring an end to your friendship. Emirati's have different words to express the relationships of paternal and maternal relatives. It is not surprising your friend did not connect the close blood relationship as being the same on her mother's side of the family. At any rate, the deed is done, not only is she powerless to stop or change it, she has probably

185

fallen in love with her husband. It would probably cause her shame to appear as the uneducated desert dweller in front of you.

B is your only option. You probably shouldn't have inquired as to her connection with her husband anyway. C is socially unacceptable. You may question a woman endlessly about her siblings, parents and children, but her relationship with her husband is a taboo subject. While a group of Emirati women in a majlis setting might talk quite candidly about marital relations and joke endlessly about them, the discussion is always general and never mentions specific examples. Women needing to discuss their personal relationships do so in private with a sister or their mother.

SITUATION THREE

You, a Western woman, invite a young Emirati woman to your home for a visit. She arrives accompanied by her older brother and her mother. The brother leaves after handing you a container of hot food and the mother sweeps grandly into your sitting room. Ignoring your sofa and lounge chairs, she settles herself on the floor and pours coffee from her very own thermos for the three of you into the coffee cups she brought along. The mother nibbles at one of the dishes you prepared, but clearly does not like it. She does not speak English and you quickly exhaust your meagre Arabic. Your apartment is hot and the mother soon doses off in an upright position.

Circle the things you would do:

- **A** Turn up the air conditioning.
- **B** Bring a bowl of water for washing.
- **C** Smile, ask your guests if they are comfortable.
- **D** Try to get the mother to sit in a chair.
- **E** Drink their coffee and eat the food they brought.
- **F** Find some floor cushions for everyone to sit on.
- **G** Encourage the mother to use your larger coffee mugs to drink out of.

H Eat the food you prepared and visit with the daughter while you wait for the mother to wake up.

I Turn on some music to fill the silence.

J See them to the door at the end of the visit.

Comments

The only responses that would be inappropriate are D, G, I, and J. In this situation it appears that the mother is ascertaining your suitability as a friend for her daughter. You want to make her as comfortable as possible and she is most comfortable on the floor. Planning ahead and already having cushions on the floor as an option would be a brilliant stroke on your part. The mother has brought her own cups because given your different beliefs, it is possible your cups at one time contained alcohol and will never quite be clean again.

The mother is probably extremely traditional and any music you possess would be offensive to her. Don't worry, she is comfortable with the silence. Ask after their comfort many times. Use the daughter as a translator to find out more about the mother. The right line of questioning might just bring out some fascinating stories. When they are ready to leave, be sure and walk them all the way to their car. Stand at the curb and wave goodbye until they are well on their way.

SITUATION FOUR

It is Ramadan and you are sitting on an empty beach with a friend eating lunch. An Arab man comes, sits down and begins chatting with you, *"Salam a lai kum – How are you?"* What do you do?

A Say, *"Wai lai kum salam – We are fine thank you, and you?"* Offer the man some food.

B Say, *"Wai lai kum salam – We are fine al-hamdulilah."* Put the food away in the icebox (cooler, chillibin).

    C Say, "Excuse me, we must go." Pack up your belongings and move to another beach.

Comments

A is an entirely inappropriate response. During Ramadan Muslims are in a heightened spiritual state. It is extremely rude to tempt the man with food and further, it is illegal for you to be caught eating in public in daylight hours during the month of Ramadan.

B is not a bad response especially if it is followed by C soon after. You should try to get the food in the icebox before the man comes close enough to see it. You are probably inappropriately dressed given the time of year and may be regarded as tempting the Arab's thoughts. Such behaviour is more the fault of the tempters than the temptees in this society.

While it is a good idea to move on, C by itself is a little abrupt. Also, you may not have any more privacy on another beach. Foreigners curtail their activities during the month of Ramadan or at least make an increased effort to keep them indoors.

SITUATION FIVE

You climb into a taxi, state your destination and sit back for the ride. The driver pulls into traffic, turns and smiles at you and begins behaving in a suggestive manner. What do you do?

    A Scream at him to stop the car, open your door slightly to indicate you are serious and jump out the instant he brings the car to a stop.

    B Ignore him.

    C Order him to stop the car, pay him and get out.

Comments

A is the only choice. Screaming will intimidate him and show him you are in charge. He will probably stop his behaviour out of fear of being reported to the police. Taxi drivers are very opposed to having a car door open while the car is in motion, it is a very effective way to bring the car to a stop and in traffic you probably aren't going fast enough for this to be dangerous.

B may indicate to him your boundaries are flexible and he should test them further.

C is awfully generous of you but why do you feel you owe him a thing?

SITUATION SIX

You, a man, and two female friends have just arrived at what you think is a great campsite. A villager sees you from afar and comes over to warn you of the danger of falling rocks on your campsite. You thank him and chat with him a bit. He wants to know the relationship of you and your two friends. You:

A Explain that you are all just friends out having a nice time. You view this as a good opportunity to educate him in your ways.

B Tell him it is a personal matter you do not wish to discuss.

C State that one of the women is your wife and the other is your sister.

Comments

A will not work. The villager, raised very traditionally, cannot understand this situation any better than you can understand the situation with his women. He probably has not had much contact with foreigners or read a book like this one. You are more likely to shock him than you are to educate him.

189

B leaves him to form his own impressions, either that you've hired the women or that you are all related. He understands what a private matter women are and may leave the topic alone. However, he sees you as an outsider and therefore not subject to his cultural rules. He may press you further. If he does, go on to answer C if you aren't already there. It is a white lie, but it is also something he can understand because sisters are a part of a man's incest group (people he can't marry) and a wife belongs to him. It is acceptable for you to be in their company.

SITUATION SEVEN

You are driving by yourself on a highway between two cities. Two young Emirati men wearing dishdashas and driving a four-wheel-drive vehicle pull up beside you. They keep abreast of you and try to get your attention. What do you do?

A Ignore them and slow your speed.

B Make rude hand gestures at them.

C Increase your speed in an effort to get away from them.

Comments

A is most likely to get them to leave you alone. Few people here like to drive slowly so the men will grow bored with their game and move on. B gives them attention, but could anger them and cause them to do something dangerous like run you off the road.

C is what they are hoping you will do – join in a game of chase. They would really like you to eventually pull over and chat with them, the catch part of the game. You can't outrun them and you might get a ticket trying. Go back to A.

SITUATION EIGHT

A male Emirati colleague gives you, a Western woman, an expensive gift of gold jewellery. You remember that to refuse a gift in this culture is rude. You:

A Thank him profusely but refuse the gift explaining that such a gift carries too much meaning in your culture.

B Thank him, accept the gift and treat it lightly.

C Thank him profusely and eagerly accept the gift.

Comments

To refuse a gift is rude. However, if the Emirati man has spent much time in a Western culture, he knows accepting his gift means accepting him too. Guage his experience and sensitivity to Westerners, if it is high, go with A. If his Western experience or sensitivity are less than proficient, go with B and proceed with caution. You might want to have less contact with the man until you are sure of his intentions and he understands yours. C suggests you are open to personal relations and that you may be willing to be intimate if enough presents are extended.

SITUATION NINE

You are a Western man sitting by yourself at a corner table of Hardees. You are minding your own business when a black cloaked woman leaves her group of female friends and approaches your table. She is lightly veiled and her face is uncovered. You can see she is exceptionally beautiful. She says hello, hands you a piece of paper with her name and telephone number written on it and says, "You will call me?" You:

A Apologise, tell her you can't do that, pack up your food and escape.

B Thank her, accept the piece of paper, extricate yourself from the situation as soon as politeness will allow and later throw the number away.

C Thank her, accept the number, chat with her a bit and call her later, maybe even setting up a time and place to meet.

Comments

A is rude and might cause the woman embarrassment in front of her friends, though her behaviour is inappropriate to begin with and would cause her shame if more people knew about it. B is the safest reaction since you allow her to save face. You will want to make the quickest exit possible because of the inappropriate nature of the situation. C is a really bad idea. The whole thing may be a set up and who is going to prevent you from disappearing?

DOS AND DON'TS

- Make friends with same gender people.

- Single women should go to bars with at least one other person. Too many unaccompanied visits will harm her reputation among even the expats.

- Travel with at least one other person whenever possible.

- Frequent the same stores for your regular shopping. The store owners will begin to know you and feel responsible for you so you will not be hassled or followed by store employees or customers.

- Don't interrupt, stare at or distract someone who is praying.

- Don't make critical remarks about any religious practice. Religious practices are respected.

- Men and women should not touch in public. It is not illegal, but it is shocking.
- Avoid discussions about Israel, alcohol, drugs, and sex.
- Enquire about family, but do not enquire about women.
- Do not wear Emirati clothing, covering your head is acceptable and appreciated but their national dress is not for you.
- Do not point the soles of your feet at another person.
- Do not use your left hand when eating.
- Accept coffee or tea whenever it is offered.
- Don't photograph people without obtaining their permission.
- Don't discuss your humble origins, you will only embarrass yourself. Don't boast of your achievements either. Fortune and unearned wealth are more greatly admired.
- Do not express dislike of a relative and do not bring up fantastic tales of a black sheep in your family. Family is respected and protected. Dirty laundry is not aired.
- Say positive things.
- Show pictures of your family. People in pictures should be adequately covered by Emirati standards.
- Don't shake hands with women. Men should allow the Emirati or Arab woman to decide if she will shake hands.
- Stand when people enter a room except if the person is a servant or tea boy.
- Accept a gift with both hands, but do not open it in front of the person who gave it to you.
- Keep pets locked up when entertaining, your guests might not like them nearly as much as you do.
- Dress conservatively in public. Women should wear dresses or skirts, men should wear loose fitting pants and be well kept.

FURTHER READING

The best books to read are usually the ones you can find easily. If you can't find information on the Emirates, you could write to the publishers below to order any books you think you might like to have. The best resource centre I've been able to find is at the Zayed library in Al-Ain where they have a special collection of books on the Emirates and Emiratis. It is quite extensive. Unfortunately you must be faculty, a student, an Emirati, or have wasta to use it.

The Arabs

Baghdad Without a Map. Tony Horwitz, 1991, Penguin Group Books. Horwitz, a mostly out of work journalist cum house-husband, recounts his tales of freelancing in the Middle East. He takes us from one country to another as he follows stories giving us humorous insight into the Arabs' thought processes and the distinctly Middle Eastern bureaucracy. I enjoyed the chapters on the Emirates and Oman the most, but can't help wondering which chapter a foreigner in Egypt would enjoy.

Understanding Arabs: A Guide for Westerners. Margaret K. Nydell, 1987, Intercultural Press Inc., Yarmouth, Maine. An accurate, straightforward guide to understanding Arabs in general. Nydell discusses family values, the position of women in business, the working environment in general, language, etc. She gives sound advice in an easy to read format.

The Arab Mind. Raphael Patai, 1983, Macmillan Publishing, NY. Patai explains Arab values for the lay person to understand and then compares them to his European ones and finds the Arabs wanting (which leaves me to think, either he doesn't really understand the Arabs or he has a hidden agenda). It is an academic book, though readable and very useful for understanding values, if one keeps in mind they are being manipulated to fit Patai's goals in the analysis.

The Emiratis

Mother Without a Mask: A Westerner's Story of her Arab Family. Patricia Holton, London, 1992, Motivate Publishing. This is a story of Holton's interaction with an Emirati family. It is told from her perspective without interpretation or analysis, leaving the reader with little more in-depth understanding of the culture than 'it is our way.' The author shies away from any in-depth questioning and while she may have told a nice story, we are not left with any real understanding of the values the Emiratis' beliefs and behaviours are based on.

The Bedouin. Shirley Kay, 1978, Crane, Russak & Co, Inc. NY. A short read on the food, clothes, housing, education, and trade of the past. The book describes the nomadic environment of a group of people on the move in search of water and how they came to be a more settled people. Sections of the book are also devoted to the traditions surrounding marriage and childbirth and to tribal and social structure.

Fatima and her Sisters. Dorothy Van Ess, 1961, The John Day Company NY. Van Ess and her husband have both published extensively on the subject of the Arab Bedouin. This book is the story of Van Ess' life among the Muslim women in Basrah, in lower Iraq, where she opened a school in 1912. She discusses the lack of progress among these women due to a polygamous society, illiteracy, and cultural beliefs regarding dress. The author sees these as heavy odds set against women and yet marvels at the vitality, humour, and lively personalities they have. She ends on an upbeat note believing that these characteristics of the women hold promise for the future.

The Bedouins of Arabia. Thierry Mauger, 1988, Souffles Creation Production, Paris. A largely photographic account of the author's travels among the Bedouin of Saudi Arabia. It is an ethnological thesis of the time he and his wife spent with the Bedouin. The author says that without his wife, he would not have been so readily accepted. He feels he captured a dying civilisation. His brilliant pictures visually portray rituals of eating, celebrating and segregation. He also captured the warriors, the art of falconry, woven products, animal husbandry, clothes, and jewellery all of which are glossed with his personal experience.

The Emirates

Persian Gulf States. Country Studies. Area Handbook Series. Edited by Helen Chapin Metz, Washington, D.C., January 1993, US Government Printing Office. This book has a chapter on the economics, politics, history, population and geography of the UAE. It is an expensive book if you are only interested in the one chapter.

History

The Origins of the United Arab Emirates. Rosemarie Said Zahlan, 1978, St. Martin's Press NY. The book begins by giving a background on traditional rule, particularly the history of internal fighting and challenges to power. It then introduces the British involvement and subsequent boundary and territory disputes with Saudi Arabia and Iran. It is in short the early history of the country that lead to the emergence of the UAE as a country.

From Trucial States to United Arab Emirates. Frauke Heard-Bey, 1982, Longman Group Ltd. London and NY. Heard-Bey gives geographical details of the Emirates and then moves on to the

Emiratis' tribal structure and history. He uses this as a basis to explain how Abu Dhabi emerged as the leading Emirate and what it means for one man to govern a tribal people. He discusses the formation of the federation in more detail than most people probably require. He gives a history of the arrival of Islam and describes the influence of Islam on daily life. Finally, he describes the traditional means of income from agriculture and trade to pearling and animal husbandry.

Food

The Complete Middle East Cookbook. Tess Mallos, 1993, London, Peter Ward Book Exports. Contains a chapter on Gulf food mentioning that many items are borrowed from other countries as a result of trade contact. The Gulf chapter opens with a good run down on dining etiquette and the importance of coffee as a symbol of Arabic hospitality.

Aesthetics and Ritual in the UAE. Aida S. Kanafani, 1983, The American University of Beirut. Aida's dissertation is an ethnographic work on food and body rituals in the Emirates. Every possible detail regarding dining and the cleansing of the body is given in more detail than most people would probably find interesting. Other topics discussed (in detail) are clothes, incense burning, and child-bearing. It is a brilliant source for anyone doing research.

Business

Dubai: The City of Opportunities 1995. A Comprehensive Manual on Investment Opportunities in Dubai – Rules and Procedures. Dubai Chamber of Commerce and Industry. Dubai, U.A.E. Just like the title says, it is comprehensive. If you want to set up a business in Dubai, this little book should be able to answer every question you have. It also gives some current economic background information and the standard historical synopsis of the country. Compiled information from chambers of commerce in the other emirates is not yet as organized or as complete.

Travelling in the UAE

Arab Gulf States: Bahrain, Kuwait, Oman, Qatar, Saudi Arabia, and the United Arab Emirates. Gordon Robison, March 1993, Lonely Planet Publications, Berkeley, CA. A guidebook advising the reader where to stay and eat and what to do. It gives a little information on each of the seven emirates in the chapter on the United Arab Emirates and gives an overview of etiquette and practical considerations for the whole Middle East in the first two chapters. A good little book to have if you are doing quick trips through several countries and have limited room in your backpack.

Women

The Women of the United Arab Emirates. Linda Ursa Soffan, 1980, London: Croam Helm, and Totowa, NJ: Barnes & Noble Books.

Women at Work. Mohammed A. Nour. Nour traces the historical position of working women in the Middle East. Considering technology as the greatest progressive force on the women's movement, he outlines four perspectives on the position of women: the fundamental, the progressive, the feminist, and the developmental views.

Arab Women: Old Boundaries, New Frontiers. Judity E. Tucker (Ed.), 1993, Indiana University Press, Bloomington and Indianapolis. This is a collection of works by 12 authors all looking at the present as a time of change for Arab women. With this thesis in mind, the authors discuss the topics of gender relations, culture, economic change, women in business, Palestinian women under Israeli occupation, feminism, politics, revolutionary politics, family, and women's contribution to literature.

Religion

Women in the Qur'an, Traditions and Interpretation. Barbara Freyer
Stowasser, 1994, Oxford University Press, Oxford and NY.
Stowasser gives an analysis of Islamic texts dealing with women
and gives insight into the place of women in Islam. She focuses on
how women's position has been interpreted. She cites great
women in Islamic history, particularly the prophet's wives whose
lives and representation in the Koran survive in traditions today.
For example, she outlines traditions which defend polygamy even
though Arabs are divided as to whether or not it should be
abolished.

Understanding Islam: an Introduction to the Muslim World. Thomas
W. Lippman, 1995, a Meridian Book published by the Penguin
Group NY. This is a clear, easy to read explanation of the founding
of Islam and a description of its growth into a great Empire that
still influences the world today. Lippman states that Islam is not
only a religious force, but also a political force and an economic
one as well. He describes the interplay between religion, government, and current events and the beliefs and practices of modern
day Islam.

The Koran (with a parallel Arabic text), translated by N. J. Dawood,
1956, 1993 edition. Dawood translates the Koran as close to the
original as English grammar and idioms will allow. The language
is flowery and there is no guide to assist the reader in understanding meaning. However, it is a good book to actually use since one
could use the Arabic in actual prayer and the English to aid
comprehension. Chapters are included by length beginning with
the longest and ending with the shortest rather than given in
chronological order.

THE AUTHOR

Gina Crocetti, an American, was born in Portland, Oregon in 1965. The daughter of an army officer, she began travelling at the age of three months and has not yet stopped. She earned her M.A. TESOL from Portland State University and her RSA TEFL Diploma from Cambridge University and has been teaching English since 1991 in the US, the United Arab Emirates, and now in Korea.

After being offered a teaching position at the UAE University she decided to find out what she could about the Emirates. At the library she discovered the UAE's proximity to Saudi Arabia, but was unable to find useful information for someone going to live there. Her purpose in writing *Culture Shock! UAE* was twofold. On the one hand, she wished to make available to others the answers to the questions she began with. On the other hand, she wanted to explore why, when she had already lived in so many different places, adjustment was so difficult there. She hopes her explanations ease the adjustment for others and fosters sensitivity between and among all groups living in the Emirates.

Ms. Crocetti has been publishing and presenting her teaching ideas internationally for the past five years. She is currently writing a textbook for teaching English to speakers of other languages and hopes to begin a novel as soon as time permits.

INDEX